PRAISE FOR
TO CRACK THE WORLD OPEN

This well written, deeply personal account of one man's struggle to find his place in the world will find a place on the shelf alongside such Alaska classics as Jonathan Raban's *Passage to Juneau* and Rockwell Kent's *Wilderness*.

—Lynn Schooler, author, photographer, outdoorsman, and Alaskan wilderness guide

A compelling and poetically written memoir about a young man running from corporate America and the impact of a neglectful and painful upbringing. Living alone with his wise and loyal dog in the remote wilds of Alaska, he contemplates, interrogates, and confronts the painful places within, and ultimately understands the transformative journey of his life.

—Anna Quinn, bestselling author of *The Night Child*

TO CRACK THE WORLD OPEN

TO CRACK THE WORLD OPEN

SOLITUDE, ALASKA, AND A DOG NAMED WOODY

WARD SERRILL

GIRL FRIDAY BOOKS

Poem by Li Po, from *Crossing the Yellow River*, translated by Sam Hamill, Tiger Bark Press. Poem by Li Shi, from *Poems of the Masters*, translated by Red Pine, Copper Canyon Press. Poem by Chuang Tsu, *Inner Chapters*, translated by Gia-Fu Feng and Jane English, Vintage Books, and Chuang Tzu, translated by Herbert A. Giles.

 GIRL FRIDAY BOOKS

Published by Girl Friday Books™, Seattle

Produced by Girl Friday Productions
www.girlfridayproductions.com

Design: Paul Barrett
Project management: Sara Spees Addicott
Editorial: Dave Valencia

Front and back cover photos: Ward Serrill
Interior photos courtesy of Ward Serrill, except where noted
Author photo: Sophie Jane Hardy

ISBN (paperback): 978-1-954854-18-5
ISBN (e-book): 978-1-954854-19-2

Library of Congress Control Number: 2021936178

First edition

To dog-loving souls and freedom seekers all . . .

You ask me why
I live alone in the mountain forest
And I smile and am silent
Until even my soul grows quiet.
It lives in the other world
The one no one owns.
The peach trees blossom.
The water continues to flow.

—Li Po

Dogs are mirrors
And mirrors, dogs
That is all ye need to know on earth
And all ye need to know.

—Dr. Woody

Love is the only way out of the box.

—Richard Buell

CONTENTS

AUTHOR'S NOTE

I describe this book as an impressionistic documentary of a period of my life. I have attempted to be attentive to the truth of my experiences while also recognizing that memory is a subjective animal. In order to tell this story, time and experiences are in places condensed and some characters are amalgamations. In order to further protect privacy, I deliberately changed the names, characterizations, and descriptions of a few people. I hope this to be as true as possible to my memory and the emotional truth of events and, in the end, an offering of healing and inspiration. I give thanks to all those who crossed my trail, both friends and those of a more challenging nature who inspired me to grow.

PROLOGUE

Behm Canal, Alaska, Fall 1983

Pssshhhwaah! The gasp from the orca's blowhole heaved somewhere ahead of us in the fog-enshrouded sea. Waves slapped the hollowness of the canoe. Woody stood up, his yellow Labrador ears poised forward. I assessed the situation: it was past midnight; we were a half mile from a shore I could no longer see; we had no light, no life preservers, no flare, nothing. Just my style—to launch off with little preparation or sense that anything could go wrong.

Pssshhhwaah! By the diffused flashes of the lighthouse through the fog, my eyes searched the dim water for a dorsal fin or a tail. Nothing. I started to count. *One . . . two . . . three . . . four . . .* and got to twelve. *Pssshhhwaah!* Enlarged by the fog, it sounded like the breath of a giant wrestler laboring uphill.

No one knew we were out here. How long could I survive in forty-six-degree water? Seven minutes? I'd make it maybe a hundred feet. Woody, though, would likely survive; or would he swim around endlessly searching for me before succumbing and joining me in the under deep?

Pssshhhwaah! Another primal exhale echoed through the night, maybe twenty-five yards away, just off the edge of the fogbank. Then I saw it. A long, straight ebony fluke arched out of the water, shimmering, six feet high above a sleek, streamlined body. An adult male. He blew a plume of mist into the still night air before descending again, heading directly toward us.

In the bow, Woody stared ahead. *Does a dog know how to pray?*

Chapter 1

A DOG WITH WINGS

Huntsville, Alabama, Fall 1964

The glass doorknob to the walk-in closet turned silently. A mysterious mélange of faded perfume, Brylcreem, and laundry soap filled the air. Downstairs in the living room, a vacuum cleaner whined and wheezed in our large, antebellum Alabama house as I closed the door behind me.

The dark of the closet wrapped itself around my seven-year-old body. I flicked on the light. To the right, atop a chest of drawers, was Mom's costume jewelry: pearl necklaces, hairpins, and gaudy clip-on earrings with clasps that closed over my fingertips. Hanging nearby were polyester blouses, wool skirts, and a silver fox stole with its hinged jaw grasping the tail.

My stealth mission took me to Dad's side of the closet where a neat row of gray and black suits, sport coats, and starched white shirts lined up like soldiers. My fingers trailed across the silky fabric of his bow ties. Furrowing through the pockets of his two overcoats brought pay dirt in the second one: a half pack of Marlboros. Two perfect tobacco cylinders slipped into my pocket.

On the way out, in the middle of Mom's dresser, I found a half dozen bras with enormous cups. Pressing them to my face, my boy-mind was overcome by their perfume. But it was incongruous; I couldn't imagine my mom or dad naked. None of us had bodies in that house. Nakedness was shameful, and anything dealing with body function was not to be mentioned. Sometimes, I would look down at my hands or feet or little-boy penis and wonder whose they were.

I felt the lace edges of a bra, and clasped and unclasped the wire hooks along the back. In the top drawer was her little black evening purse for dress-up events. I pulled out a dollar, a couple quarters, and a dime and stuffed them in my pocket, careful to leave enough change to mask the theft.

The door suddenly ripped open. "What in the name of God are you doing?" my mom shouted.

She had an armful of laundry that she threw on the bed, and then she grabbed me by the wrist and dragged me into the bedroom.

"I was looking for—" I sputtered, quickly thrusting my free hand into my pocket to cover the cigarettes.

"You know better than that!" she scolded and walloped me on the backside. I pretended it hurt. She spanked as hard as she could, but both of us knew it was having little effect. She was a small woman and not strong. Her impotence and frustration built as she wailed away, face red and kitchen apron twisted around her body.

"You used to be such a good little boy. What's gotten into you?"

I had no answer, and felt a locust cloud of guilt descending. She could pierce me so easily.

"Go to your room until your father comes home!"

Her words struck fear into my heart, and I rounded the corner to my room as fast as possible. My room was the only refuge in this large house. I felt most safe there. Sitting on my bed against the wall and counting the World War II model airplanes hanging from ceiling strings calmed me. The P-51 Mustang with its shark-mouth insignia, the twin-fuselage P-38 Lightning, and the bombers—the B-24 Liberator and the Boeing B-17—that my dad had helped design. I liked how they slowly twirled on invisible currents. The room was permeated with the smell of model paint and glue.

The only sounds in the house were lonely ones—outside the window, nuthatches and robins caroled in the fall leaves of the oaks and maples in our wooded yard. Cicadas chanted low, and crickets had begun their evening song.

Dad's '62 Impala droned up the street, pulled into the driveway, and shut down. A car door opened and slammed, and his black wing tips clacked along the walkway, up the cement steps to the porch. Mom's subdued voice met him at the door. His responses were low and monosyllabic. I heard the coat closet door open and my father hang up his overcoat. A moment later, in the kitchen, ice clinked into a glass. Then silence.

I stashed the cigarettes and money in a secret box under my bed. Time dripped like a slow-leaking faucet. The cicadas raised their din . . . then came steps, slow footfalls up the stairs and down the hall. My door opened. He never knocked.

An enormous bear filled my doorway. Five foot eleven, 205 pounds, my father stood with bow tie undone, in a white short-sleeved shirt, a crew cut, and scotch in hand. It was always better if it was his first glass.

He took a sip of his drink. Inevitably, like a ritual, he said the same thing. "Do you want to tell me about it?" It wasn't really a question. It never mattered what I said.

"I was looking for Aspergum," I said, my voice shaking.

He continued to look at me for what seemed an eternity and then just walked away. I got up and followed him downstairs.

He preferred the middle of the living room, where he pulled up a chair and sat. He turned me around, pulled my pants down, and bent me over his knee.

"I only do this because I love you," he said.

Dishes clattered in the kitchen, and the aroma of meat loaf and potatoes wafted in the air. Dad smelled of pipe smoke, alcohol, and Mennen Skin Bracer. His hand was iron. Sucking all my butt muscles inside, I counted the squares on the living room carpet and took the hits. I would not cry. "Emotions are to be submerged," he liked to say.

Sent to my room without dinner, I grabbed the secret box from under my bed and climbed out the window onto the first-story roof. Toward the backyard, it was a thirty-foot drop to the pine woods, making the roof a good place to count my loot: three dollars, sixty-five cents. I pulled out a cigarette and rolled it around in my fingers and then scratched a wooden match along a shingle, illuminating a small circle around me. I had learned to inhale and sometimes did so without coughing. Like Dad, I was a Marlboro man.

Adrift in a sea of strangers, alone on a small raft, I smoked my distress. I smoked my hatred of them. Smoked a rage that wanted to land a giant foot on this house, leaving only splinters behind. I smoked myself into a numb haze and floated outside my body. My hands pressed to the shingles for fear of rolling off.

The fireflies had begun their alluring semaphore between the dark trees. I tried to count their blinks. It was time for my friend to appear; the fireflies always announced his arrival. And there he came, reliably, all black and white, with a pair of quick wings landing next to me. My invisible dog friend, Oreo. I put my arm over him and climbed onto his back. He lifted off and I held on to his neck. The cool night air whisked by my face, and Oreo carried me, through the pines, into the starry sky, free, free, free . . .

Chapter 2

BOXTOWN

Fall 1981

I was twenty-four years old, my lungs straining against a pin-stripe vest. Twenty-seven floors below, people crossing Seneca Street looked like tiny black bugs. The ventilation system in my office hissed white noise, an ever-ceaseless whisper meant to cool, to calm, to pacify. It turned my brain to cloud. The Seattle sky was blue and untouched. In the building across the street, rows of suited figures sat at desks a quarter mile above the earth, in a box. *Boxtown.*

The adding machine whirred as I pushed the Total key. The number matched the pencil-marked spreadsheet in front of me—long-term debt, accounts payable, reserve for accumulated depreciation, debits and credits—all adding up. Next to my desk stood rows of CPA manuals and audit papers for an oil company, a bank, a winery, a truck manufacturer. These numbers stuffed in folders on shelves—the hieroglyphics of my culture—were what I had to show from the raw clay of my life's work: an ordered world in ledgers that made sense, at least on paper.

To the south, towering over the horizon, stood Mount Rainier—the Fuji of the Puget Sound, stupendously beautiful, aloof, serene, and otherworldly. Two western gulls outside my window navigated the air currents like master acrobats. Soaring as high as the Space Needle, the closest gull looked at me with a fierce yellow eye that radiated a strong, instinctual freedom. He then tilted his feathers to fall serenely away into the endless sky toward the sea.

The hallway intercom bleated, making me jump: "Mr. Serrill, see Armin McDermott . . . Mr. Serrill, Armin McDermott, please." Armin, one of the firm's partners, would want the financials for the medical supply company I was struggling over. I tossed on my suit coat and headed toward his office, but suddenly turned instead toward the back door to the hallway and made a beeline for the elevator. Nervous to be seen, I pushed the Down button every few seconds until the bell finally dinged. Once the doors closed behind me, safe inside the small box, I reveled in the feeling of falling from space, tumbling out of the sky like a seagull. A slight tickle rose in my belly as the elevator slowed and opened to the lobby.

I was really good at running away.

My destination was Pioneer Square, the old part of Seattle, five blocks south where a small urban park hid a shimmering thirty-foot waterfall—my refuge. The waterfall made a soft whisper, *sshhhhwwweeeeeeeshhhh*, like ice being shaved, as it spilled across a tumble of large brown stones. Mist and a cool breeze brushed my face and closed eyelids. The crystalline sound of the falls seeped through me and washed away Boxtown's files and accounts and confusions.

The waterfall made me sleepy, and I wanted to stay wrapped in its soft folds, but the pressure to be "billable" carried me away. I reluctantly rejoined the funeral procession back into the black monolith of the Seafirst Building. In the lobby, an older man followed me into the elevator. He turned to face the door and stood a foot in front of me as the box whirred and ascended. We didn't speak or acknowledge each other. His neck skin rolled over his collar like a raspberry donut. The change in his pocket jangled, and his breaths were shallow and quick. The elevator slowed, the bell dinged, and he walked out, still fingering his pocket change.

A short *whoosh* later, and the door opened to the twenty-seventh floor. Before me stood one of my supervisors, Tev Renton.

"What are you looking at?" he sneered with a crooked smile. Renton was tall and lean with short blond hair. I froze.

"I don't know what I'm looking at," I said, faking nonchalance, trying to maneuver my way past him. Renton wasn't much older than me, but he took a dogged pleasure in terrorizing junior accountants. He was very good at it, a master of veiled loathing and subtle menace. But the moment you took it seriously, he would shift the aggression to fraternal laughter as if it were all a joke, and you got a slap on the back. If you ever challenged him directly, he'd cut you to pieces before you knew what hit you. The only way into Renton's graces was to go out drinking with him—slam down shots after work. Drinking was the sport of choice among the Boxtown accountants.

"It's just tough being inside on a day like this," I ventured. The elevator doors began to close, and he stopped them with his foot.

"Oh, and you're just too good to be in here with the rest of us?" he said in a kidding way.

"Yeah, yeah," I said, smiling as I squeezed past him, relieved by the moment of lightness. He stepped into the elevator and turned back with a grin frozen on thin lips.

"Eat shit," he said with quiet venom as the doors closed.

"Ah, Mr. Serrill, I've been looking for you!" I jumped. From behind me, out of the restroom, came Armin McDermott. With a paternal smile, he put his arm over my shoulders and rushed me down the hallway to his office like time was money.

"Sit down, sit down," Armin said, ushering me inside. I sat across his wide wooden desk covered with folders and audit papers. CPA certificates and paintings of geometric modern art graced the walls. Through the high, shaded windows, a golden pathway of sun diamonds shimmered across Elliott Bay and glanced against the side of my face.

Armin was born in a three-piece suit. He was tall and lanky and had a friendly, folksy manner. As he moved some folders aside, he began to talk with great interest about a night-light he had found in a catalogue.

"It comes attached to a little pad of paper," he said. "In the middle of the night, if I get an idea about a tax or accounting problem, I can turn on the light and write it down." He was very pleased. I could imagine Armin in his matching pajamas, scribbling down thoughts about a company's contingent liability on long-term debt, then settling back into measured snores for the rest of the night.

Armin's voice was soothing and metronomic. I had to fight back a sleepiness from my visit to the waterfall and the adrenaline crash following the encounter with Renton. The sunlight warming the side of my face didn't help matters.

"Jason Wilcox from Physio called me," Armin said, getting down to business. "They had a large shipment of heart defibrillators in transit at year end that's not on the books." He glanced at me over his wire-rimmed reading glasses. "I assured him we would have caught that?" he asked rhetorically, fixing me with his pencil-point blue eyes. To have missed it would mean hundreds of thousands of dollars in error in the financial statements I was doing.

"Oh, yeah, sure," I said. "Sure." But I wasn't. In fact, I had the sinking feeling I had blown it. The white noise of the ventilator was making it hard to concentrate.

"Good, good, I thought so," Armin said. He began rattling on in his train-track monotone about how vital this client was and how the biotech field was growing rapidly in the Puget Sound area. After some moments, he said, "There is something else I want to talk to you about."

I blinked to wake up and straightened in my seat. "Sure," I said.

"It's about a new client . . ." But my mind started to wander. I nodded mechanically to let him know I was still listening, but was quickly losing the battle to stay awake. Time droned on—then a word he spoke hit me like a cold glass of water in the face.

"Alaska?" I repeated, blinking.

Armin stopped, puzzled that I would interrupt him.

"Yes," he said, "Alaska. It's a small village corporation outside of Ketchikan. I think we might have a few more of these clients before too long." He was talking about corporations in Alaska Native villages, newly formed by something called the Alaska Native Claims Settlement Act.

My hand shot up reflexively. "I'll take all of those."

Armin looked at me with my arm raised as if I had beamed in from the starship *Enterprise*. He couldn't comprehend such impulsiveness. How could I make a decision if I had yet to hear the facts?

How could he understand the word he had just uttered had pierced me so unexpectedly? How it had infused me with a sudden promise of wildness, hinting toward a mystery, calling me into an unbound future. Those three syllables, *Alaska*, had put me on the back of a dog with wings, flying north over Puget Sound on a pathway of sun diamonds across the sea.

Chapter 3

INTO A NEW LAND

Spring 1982

Surrounded by my rectangular audit bags, I lay on a lounge chair on the back deck of the Alaska State Ferry. The air was clear and sea-scrubbed. Armin McDermott was sending me up to a remote Native village in Southeast Alaska to audit their new corporation—a dream come true.

People camping on the deck for the forty-hour ride to Ketchikan sat around tents in the late-afternoon setting sun, chatting quietly, eating, or reading. A guy on guitar softly sang "Friend of the Devil." The air tanged of tide pools and diesel smoke. We passed mile after mile of forested coast between Vancouver Island and the mainland—shores punctuated by narrow strips of sand or outcrops of barnacled rock. Backlit by the sun, rounds of kelp, the color of molasses, swirled in currents. Seabirds cried. Now and again, a lone cabin or small village appeared. On rocks, a half dozen sea lions snoozed.

Following along in the ferry's wake, Dall's porpoises raced and leapt.

What enchanted world was this? Drunk on sea breeze and beauty.

The charm came crashing down the next night at eleven as we pulled into the industrial heap of Ketchikan, Alaska's First City. Rock and busted machinery lined the waterway. A desolate road ran below tree-denuded hillsides. Yellow lights cast shadows on an empty parking lot. The scene did not fit my vision of raw, wild Alaska.

I grabbed one of the last rooms at The Landing, a roadside hotel. In the bar, a roomful of locals was getting plastered while Reagan bleated away on TV about the great threat Nicaragua posed to our democracy. I had a three-dollar can of Bud, ate some greasy fish-and-chips, and well past midnight, made it up to my room, eventually falling into a fitful sleep.

At two in the morning, yelling and screaming shocked me awake. A crash of glass. My heart knocking like a diesel engine, I flicked on the light. The voices were coming from the room next door, slightly muffled by the cheap walls.

"*You fucking asshole!* I hate your fucking guts!" a woman screamed. Another crash of glass.

"Shut up, bitch!" a man roared.

"Leave me alone!" she yelled back. Another glass smashed against the wall.

Despite my pounding on the paneling, the slurred argument from the two lovebirds continued the rest of the night.

At dawn, I piled my audit bags into a Cessna 185, and we were soon above the rock-strewn town, twelve cylinders *rap-a-papping* against my sleep-deprived cranium. A flock of seagulls jumped out of our way, and below us, a seiner unzipped the channel, leaving behind two strings of silver beads that shone in the morning sun. A small ferry, resembling a floating

Birkenstock sandal, chugged across the Narrows from the airport.

As the floatplane's engine settled into its rhythm, I began to relax a bit. We flew north and west across Clarence Strait. After a half hour, on Prince of Wales Island, we curled into Kasaan Bay, the northernmost of Haida villages on the coast. The plane's pontoons hissed as they touched water and dragged us gently to settle. The pilot steered to the end of the dock, stepped out, and unloaded my bags. In one fluid motion, he waved, shoved off, and climbed back into his seat. Soon, the plane was thrumming its way like a large horsefly into the blue morning sky, banking behind a silhouette of trees on the point.

I stood alone on a long dock that led to a crescent-moon beach. A hillside of tall spruce, cedar, and hemlock trees ringed the driftwood-littered sands below. Other than a sun-washed shack here and there, the place seemed deserted.

A bald eagle, prehistoric looking in the radiant day, slowly lifted from a moss-covered limb and flew toward the sea. A seal popped up its head and stared at me in my white button-down shirt and holding two audit bags. It blinked once slowly and then slipped back into the bay. From somewhere, a raven made a sound like a knock on a large wooden door that echoed off the surrounding hillside.

Something hit me right then between my eyeballs: a pure-ness and startling clarity from this *gourmet* air and water of Alaska. A lucid brilliance infiltrated my soul and spoke to a primal part of me wooed by wild beauty. Something I had been seeking all my life called to me: the simple freedom of just being here, immersed in untamed nature without a building or piece of concrete in sight.

From the far side of the bay, a four-wheel ATV came out of the forest and slowly made its way along the beach, bumping over stray drift logs. It rolled across to the dock and putted out to me. At the handlebars sat a man with a white crew cut.

"Hi," he said, smiling. "I'm Edwin. Pile on." Edwin, it turned out, was the president of the Haida company I had come to audit. Bounding along on the back of the ATV on an Alaskan beach, I wrapped my arms around his waist to keep from falling off.

"You come at a good time," Edwin yelled to me. "There's a party, a potlatch."

We pushed our way into the woods down a dirt street past some Bureau of Indian Affairs stick-frame homes, wet sopped by the endless rains and beaten by too many winters. Kids on bikes stared at me. We passed a sun-grayed totem, an eagle at its top with a beaver and salmon below, near a cedar tribal house that seemed to wear the ghosts of the past like an old blanket.

This Alaska land held darkness, adventure, and danger; and something in me needed it. My days in Boxtown were tolling to an end.

Chapter 4

THE LITTLE RED CABIN

March 1983

A slow *galunk-galunk* of waves slapped against the hull. I woke in a bunk of a houseboat in Ketchikan's Bar Harbor as wintry light undulated on the wall of the cramped berth. A damp smell of mildew permeated the frozen air. Inside my sleeping bag, something warm slept in the crook of my arm—a twelve-week-old puppy's chest rose and fell. I didn't want to move.

With $850 left to my name, I had quit Boxtown to start a new life on this rocky island in Southeast Alaska. Ketchikan made sense as the base camp from which to launch my escape. It was known to me from my work with various Native corporations in the area.

But I wasn't prepared to come to Alaska alone. An ad in the *Seattle Times* for yellow Labrador hunting dogs sealed my fate. Woody—named after Guthrie—was of champion bloodline and seemed ready for any adventure.

Ketchikan was a squalid logging, tourist, and fishing town of fourteen thousand people. It sported twenty-six churches and twenty-seven bars—an institutional rivalry that played out every weekend. The bars had a decided advantage: more customers and open twenty-three hours a day. Drinking holes closed only an hour daily from five to six in the morning to mop out the floors. Drunks napped along the sidewalks until the bars opened again.

Our houseboat was far from charming, a 1960s factory-built fiberglass job. It had rocked and molded away in the incessant rains here: thirteen feet a year, 234 days' worth. For weeks, despite the wetness, I reveled in our private sanctuary, letting the endless deluge begin to rock away the confusions of my three-piece-suit masquerade. Away from the force field of a family I didn't belong in, away from boxes, away from the noise of freeways and jets and the ringing of phones.

We couldn't hide out any longer, though. The owner of the houseboat wanted it back. I needed a new place to live. A woman at a bar told me about an abandoned cabin north of town. Going out there would be a good mission for the day. Woody grunted and rolled out of my arms, trailing a warm waft of milk-puppy smell. I pulled on a pair of pants as cold as frozen pasta and ate a bowl of cereal for breakfast while Woody sucked up his puppy chow.

The dock was covered in frost. Backlit by the dawn sun, it glistened like blue, silver, and red fur. Woody crunched over the dock with delight, snuffling his nose into the ice crystals. Tail wagging, he explored ropes tied to seiners and skiffs, buckets, nets, and shore-power outlets. He took in the mélange of fish kill, swabbed decks, drunk heavings, and the biography of every dog who had peed there in the past month.

At the top of the ramp, I scraped the ice off the windshield of a rented beater VW Rabbit with a piece of broken PVC pipe. The engine pinged to life, and we drove out of town on a two-lane road that clung to the hillside. Woody delighted in the cold Alaskan air, his black nose poking out the passenger window. We passed the Louisiana-Pacific pulp mill, belching its gray refuse into the sky. Farther up the road was Mud Bight, a cove of a half dozen ramshackle cabins on rafts, grounded on the tide flats. Twice a day, the shacks rose and fell with the sea.

Thirteen miles out, at South Point Higgins Road, we turned off the highway and dipped and curled our way downhill toward the unseen ocean. Around a corner, a Norwegian elkhound popped its head out of the bushes and appraised Woody malevolently. A few turns later, I found the unmarked pullout in the trees.

The poignant stillness of the raw forested day felt tangible in the air. A wooden ramp descended into dark woods with a steep drop on either side that I carefully picked my way down. Woody confidently followed behind. At the bottom, across the mucky ground, a series of moss-laden boards formed a path between fifty-year-old hemlocks. Succumbing to the inevitable rain-forest decay, the planks were tilted at odd angles and heights.

Around a bend, the sound of the ocean swished through the trees and stopped me in my tracks. It touched some hidden tidal flow inside me, a mysterious ebbing and flowing contrary to clocks or spreadsheets or generally accepted accounting principles.

I took the first deep, true breath of my life.

The sun flashed through the trees while a breeze jostled the hemlock branches, part of the larger play of forest bowing and swaying with the wind around me. The rhythm of this green-limbed dance of bush, leaf, and tree merging with the sound of the surf erased past and future and moved me slowly forward as if under an enchantment.

Around one more bend and down a hill appeared the cabin, a crooked and faded wine-red shack. Its roof hung low like a hat pulled down over the outline of a shadowy eye. Woody galloped to the back porch. The door was unlocked, and soon, we found ourselves inside a small, rough kitchen with an oil stove to one side. A rusted cast-iron frying pan lay in the sink. I tried the faucet. Nothing.

The kitchen opened to a main room, about ten by twenty feet, littered with detritus from some beer-canned transient. It smelled of slightly rotted wood dried to sweetness by the sun. Porn magazines were strewn about the wood floor. There was a moldy cotton sleeping bag, a red vinyl recliner, and a cloth-covered couch gone bad. The sound of waves rustled in. It felt slightly dangerous to be there. I kept expecting to hear footsteps down the trail.

The cabin was perched twenty feet above a black reef. The primary source of light was a picture window the shape of a Nikon viewfinder, which perfectly framed the trees and the sea beyond. A beat-up picnic table stood unsteadily on a rickety porch.

A mile out to sea, a lighthouse spun its silent, persistent orb of radiance. Over the next few years, that spark and flash would settle me and sometimes frighten me as it filled the pitch-dark of the cabin with a Hitchcockian blaze before sinking everything once more into complete blackness. In storm or snow, depression or joy, ache and pain, the lighthouse was to become my steady companion on sleepless nights.

Wagging his tail slowly, Woody stood in the center of the room, looking out to sea.

The Little Red Cabin had found us.

Chapter 5

TICKING AT THE
BOTTOM OF THE SEA

Spring 1983

Against the black reef, the ocean swelled and fell with a *fizzle* and *pop*. From the forest, a varied thrush blew its high, twilight whistle once. Across the sea, smoke-blue mountains tacked down the horizon, and across a burnt-orange sky, a few clouds still ripe with light wandered about in their own good time. The Little Red Cabin, our new home, stood behind me, above the beach, surrounded by evergreens.

My drinking water came from a creek five miles away; a battered-up outhouse, the extent of my comforts. More than a dozen feet of rain a year would dump on this rugged coast, and the windchill in the winter would hit twenty-five below. Standing there on the edge of the sea, twenty-six years old and thrilled for the adventure.

No one knows where I am.

My father's gold watch read 5:17. He had given it to me as a present to celebrate my accounting job in Boxtown. A career in accounting was something he seemed to understand, unlike anything else about me. As the next wave rose against the reef, I threw the watch into the sea. It made a small *plop* and fell, pendulum-like, into the depths. It dropped through silken strands of kelp and tumbled against acorn barnacles and razor clams. It sank past orange-tipped starfish and iridescent sea urchins. Spawning cohos peered at it with bulging eyes as it slipped through the glossy hairs of seagrass and ultimately settled in the sand. Sixty feet below, crabs tap-danced over its glass face while it wound down its last pressurized beats.

I was done with clock time, done with city time and rush hour time. *Now* was the time of animals, trees, and water. I turned from the sea and headed back toward the Little Red Cabin, up its rickety stairs onto the sagging porch and over the stump for a doorstep, and went inside. Out the window of my remote outpost, the lighthouse whirled and blazed, a crack of white lightning in the center of the sea, beating back the encroaching dark.

Our cabin was a quarter mile through the woods from the dirt road. There was no telephone, no radio, only a futon mattress, a chair, and a lamp. I crawled over to my only companion asleep on the floor and watched his small chest rising and falling, punctuated by light snores. The rhythm of my own breath settled into his. Woody's presence whispered a quiet confidence into me. With him here, I could make my stand and explore a lifelong, deep-felt impulse toward freedom. To free myself of the constraints that had made me a stranger in my country, my family, and my own body. With Woody here, I could endure the endless rains and let the wild beauty of this coast have its way with me.

Everything still new and perfect about him: his black nose glistened; the pads of his paws were soft; his eyes were encircled by a swirl of vanilla hair. He dreamed deeply—of what? Of his mother, or siblings left behind? It swept across me like a wave then, a revelation: that for the first time in my life, another creature was dependent on me. It generated a tender feeling of . . . belonging. I felt the awful, sweet burden of commitment, the poignant press of having to care for him.

The lighthouse flashed white against the walls of our darkening room.

I wondered, Did my own father ever feel anything like this when he looked down at me? I imagined him baffled and afraid, but not showing it, clueless about what a man raised with knuckles and scotch was supposed to do with another infant. Maybe he felt resentment? Four kids to feed now, a job that was killing him, and a wife he didn't know how to love. As nurses bundled me away, he went off to work, a Boeing engineer with his crew cut, bow tie, white shirt, and antidepressant pharmaceuticals—a man of his time.

Woody's eyes opened and looked up at me. In those carrot-colored orbs flowed a pureness, a life force, a gladness to be with me in this wild place. I was here to listen to my own heartbeat, to learn what it was to face the elements, raw and alone with him—to crack the world open.

Chapter 6

RAIN

April 1983

It rained for twenty-seven days straight. Yet the constant deluge gave me comfort. The sound of steady rain on the roof promotes an inner life; it brings the sky down for a cup of tea. The rains felt safe and freed me to engage in my newfound solitude with no interruptions. Without a phone and no one knowing where we were, I was free from even the most benign of social obligations. Disappearing into wild beauty and studying the ways of a small dog in a raw land became my work.

Woody was my long-nosed portal into an understanding of creaturehood, a model of how to encounter the world—as far as I could tell—free from thought. He seemed to live in a continuous stream of sense awareness, following his nose, eyes, ears, and tongue into a way of life that perfectly suited his surroundings. He was always content and faced each moment with unbridled attention.

But I didn't have the leisure to fully idle about the Little Red Cabin in sense awareness. Daily-life problems had come to call. After finding the absentee owner and renting the place for $250 a month, I had to get electricity hooked up, clear downed trees, and haul water. After a day of intense cleaning, the twenty-year-old refrigerator still worked. I tried to get the oil stove going, but after it exploded and blew the cast-iron vent three feet into the air, a Coleman camp stove became a better option.

Heating the place was a work in progress; it had a lousy stone fireplace that mostly funneled smoke back into the cabin. My meager scrounging of damp wood from the forest didn't help, so a blanket and comforter over a sleeping bag and a warm dog under the covers became standard procedure. All in all, this should have been a bit miserable, but the thrill of my newfound sovereignty filled me with a deep-felt satisfaction.

The rain was continuous yet not monotonous. Soft *yin rains* came, invisible to the eye and slowly saturating all. *Horizontal rains* propelled by southeast winds whipped against the window. Sometimes, steady *grim rains* seemed to arise from an endless darkness. Small, *plopping rains* built into a clatter on the roof before softening again. There was the rain that ran down the backs of northern pintails, rain that bounced high in puddles, and rain that seemed shot from a Gatling gun. There was the rain that glittered in the limbs of the spruce and cedar, rain that made intricate circles in tide pools, and rain that tickled my naked spine as I stood bare to the world. Southeast Alaska's downpours were softening my edges in the same way water would wear down boulders in a stream.

I scored a job as controller of a Native village corporation in Saxman, south of Ketchikan. The company, Cape Fox, had been a client for a couple years while in Boxtown. I had hoped to be done with accounting, but the offer came my way, and not too many alternatives presented themselves.

Off to my first day of work, I walked the crooked path through the tangled forest to the Rabbit, fired up its gravel-in-a-can diesel, and began the forty-five-minute drive to Saxman. Woody would stay at the red cabin. We had been inseparable for the last two months. An open seaside door would allow him to get outside, and new chicken wire framing the porch would keep him there.

The road to Ketchikan had been blasted out of rock and steep hills, following the craggy coastline like a string. Eleven miles in, I passed the LP mill, the town's major employer, appearing apocryphal as it pumped its belch into low-hanging clouds. The federal government had signed a sweet-heart fifty-year deal with LP, guaranteeing a steady supply of old-growth trees practically free, from the Tongass—the largest national forest in the country—to be made into disposable baby diapers, coffee cups, and cigarette filters.

In town, the Rabbit zipped by Creek Street, the former whorehouse boardwalk, and then Thomas Basin with its seiners, gillnetters, and long-liners. At Tatsuda's grocery, the last stop south of town, I pulled over to pick up a hitchhiker.

Frank David was Tlingit, from Saxman, with jet-black hair and the sharp features of a bird of prey. His tired eyes were muddy and bloodshot, the whites tinged yellow. He wore a white football jersey with orange lettering, wet from the rain. A sweet gut-rot smell of alcohol permeated the car as he got in. Immediately, I tensed up.

"Where you headin'?" I asked.

"Up ahead," Frank answered in a high, enthusiastic voice, pointing down the road. "Come to Tatsuda's for some pop." He laughed raggedly as he pulled a Mickey's Big Mouth out of a bag and cracked it open.

I was on edge as we pulled out. It never goes away, the wariness around drinkers, waiting for the other foot to come down.

"You wanta beer?" he asked.

"Nah, thanks. I'm on my way to work. First day. Cape Fox." Two ravens flew across the road. A slate-gray seiner chugged its way up the Tongass Narrows.

"Cape Fox," he said. "My uncle Jack was the leader of Alaska Native Brotherhood. He started Cape Fox." He polished off the Mickey in a long slug, and we drove in silence for a bit.

"Lived here my whole life," Frank said. A sign read *Entering Saxman, Population 356.* He cracked a second beer. "I like you," he said. "You're a nice fella. I can see that."

I wasn't sure what to say.

"Over here," Frank said. "This is my place." I pulled over beside a tumbled-down house, gray-stained from rain. A '68 Pontiac with blown tires rusted in the yard. Across the street stood a rotting totem pole with a killer whale on top. It had a small alder tree growing out of it. "You're a nice fella," he said again, not moving from his seat.

"Um, thanks . . . yeah," I said curtly, staring straight ahead. He reached over and grabbed the red Cape Fox cap off my head and put it on.

"I'm a shareholder," he said, smiling, toothless in front, with a couple black stubs at the side. He might have been thirty years old. "You work for my corporation," he said, then took another slug from his beer. "You work for me."

I had no idea what to do. The Rabbit's engine pinged and knocked. He smiled and then got out of the car, my cap still on his head, and shut the door behind him. Pulling out south down the highway, my breath shallow, I drove right by the Cape Fox office and was a quarter mile down the road before realizing it. I turned back into the parking lot and sat in the Rabbit for a spell. Eventually, I got out just as another car pulled into the lot.

The CEO, Dave Sisewell, met me at the front door. Dave was in his midfifties, a burly, squat man with a large head; a vast white beard; and an easy smile. He could have played Santa Claus in a school play. Dave brimmed with charisma and confidence. I liked him and had believed in him from the day we'd met two years earlier while I'd been auditing the company.

Behind me up the walkway came an elderly Native Alaskan woman with a cane. She moved her ample body with a slow, regal bearing. Her hair was gray and so were her eyes, and she wore a beaded vest with a raven on the lapel. A middle-aged Tlingit man, who I assumed was her son, accompanied her. They preceded us into the building and sat down in the reception area.

"Ah, Delores, this is Ward Serrill, the new controller," said Dave congenially. She did not acknowledge my presence. "This is Bobby," Dave said. "The vice chairman." Bobby, whose name was Robert Strong, had a football linebacker's build and met me with a quick, strained smile. He distractedly shook my hand.

"We come about elders' firewood," he said to Dave.

Sisewell looked surprised. "Didn't Patches deliver it?" he asked with kind exasperation as he glanced at Delores.

"No, we didn't get nothin'," Delores said, looking away.

"Ahhhh!" Dave exclaimed. "I'll get him to bring some today. And if he doesn't, you call me, okay, and I'll bring it over myself."

"That would be okay," Delores answered with stately diffidence. After a brief silence, her son helped her up, and she moved in her own unhurried way toward the door.

Dave led me through the boardroom and into his office, shutting the door behind us.

"Delores runs the village." He chuckled as he sat behind his large desk. "She's the matriarch of the largest family, the

Strongs. The town council and leaders are men, but nothing happens here if she doesn't go along with it."

"And sometimes," I said, "the CEO of a multimillion-dollar corporation has to deliver her firewood."

"It's in my job description," he said, adding his distinctive, room-filling cackle.

Dave showed me around the building and downstairs to my office. To my delight, it overlooked a creek in the woods. The presence of moving water was never far away on this island of rain. Sisewell left me to settle in and ponder over the desk in front of me. There was a stack of folders, each representing a raft of logs to be loaded onto a Japanese ship.

Cape Fox was just beginning to clear-cut large swaths of its lands for Japanese multinational companies that were buying up Alaskan old growth as fast as it could be downed. It was like the Wild West in Southeast Alaska; the market was high, and bucketfuls of cash had begun to flow. Many villages in Southeast Alaska that were surrounded by pristine forests were experiencing this boom. Saxman, with unemployment near 45 percent, and very little economic development over the past fifty years, suddenly boasted an industrial presence.

Despite the influx of cash, and new vehicles and equipment chugging around, non-Natives held all the principal jobs at Cape Fox, save one. The shareholders were struggling to understand the new corporate entity, which they were told they owned. Nine shareholders had been elected to its board of directors, none of whom at the time had executive business experience or college degrees. They did, however, have a charismatic leader in Dave Sisewell, who seemed to know what he was doing.

Cape Fox was one of 225 new corporations formed because of oil and the Alaska Native Claims Settlement Act (ANCSA), which Richard Nixon signed into law in 1973. Enormous fields of black gold had been discovered beneath Prudhoe Bay in

1969. The government wanted to build an eight-hundred-mile pipeline from the North Slope to an ice-free port in Valdez so it could fuel the legions of oversized cars and trucks in the Lower 48.

Strategically, the Alaskan Natives, seven distinct tribes overall, blocked the pipeline in court. And so, after a hundred years of inaction, the US government suddenly expressed deep concern over their moral obligation to settle indigenous land claims with Alaska Natives.

ANCSA split Alaska into twelve geographic areas, each assigned a regional corporation. Within these twelve regions, over two hundred local village corporations like Saxman's were formed as autonomous organizations. Overnight, villagers not a generation out of a subsistence lifestyle were told they were now shareholders of a profit-making corporation. These companies were collectively given deeds to hundreds of thousands of acres of land and millions of dollars.

The oil companies got their pipeline.

It was a rare and strange kind of social experiment. Take a people who had historically held in common the rights to particular resources such as areas for fishing, berry picking, hunting, and habitation, and overnight superimpose a new kind of organization where everyday villagers were handed a piece of paper worth a hundred shares of stock and told the corporation now owned the resources.

In Southeast Alaska, the corporations were given land that happened to include some of the greatest timberlands in the world—boundless temperate forests of spruce, cedar, and hemlock; trunks that five people could link arms around, rising hundreds of feet to the sky; trees that Japanese timber companies salivated over.

Alaskan Natives were about to become voracious loggers.

My job today was to verify the total board footage of logs loaded onto the Japanese ship and prepare an invoice. Alaska had invited me to its incomparable beauty, and here I was converting its primeval forests into numbers. Boxtown was pioneering its way everywhere—with me still its accomplice.

Out the forest window, the cedar-tinged brown creek meandered through. Bright-yellow skunk cabbage sprouted in the wet soil along its banks, a few munched by black bears just out of hibernation.

In the afternoon, Dave took me on a tour of Cape Fox facilities, starting with the sawmill he was building in Ward Cove across from the LP mill. I felt awkward in my oxford shirt shaking hands with logging men and supervisors in Carhartts and mud-caked boots. A fleet of log loaders, D6 Cats, boom boats, dump trucks, transports, and pickups caterwauled and tracked through the diesel-mired mud, puffing plumes of blue smoke in the air. It was exciting and appalling, the ways of men's commerce on a mission to extract resources from the land as fast as it could. A group of bankers showed up, and Dave gave them all red Cape Fox hats and stood on a pile of logs broadcasting his dream of a Native-owned sawmill he was building—and for which he needed loans, big loans.

On the way back to the office, Dave drove me along winding streets behind Ketchikan and up a hill to a locked gate. On the other side was another of Dave's dreams, a seventeen-acre rock hilltop above the town that he had blasted and bulldozed flat. Dave spoke energetically about his vision of a grand hotel overlooking the Tongass Narrows. He was just waiting, he said, for the financing. Dave brimmed with deep pockets of charismatic self-confidence. It all seemed a bit much, and I wondered how much the shareholders understood what he was doing.

At the end of the day, the rain pouring steady, I drove the gloomy, long road home. Excited to see Woody after our first day apart, I bounded down the crooked boardwalk to the red cabin, flung the door open, and yelled, "Hey, buddy!"

The cabin was empty. I raced out to the porch. Over in the corner was a puppy-size hole diligently scratched through the chicken wire. I ran back through the woods, sick at heart, searching the dirt roads near the cabin for a mile on each side. With but a cupful of light remaining to the day and a hard rain falling, I kept looking in the ditches with a fear that he would be there, cast aside from an F-150 tire tread. Maybe he had been plucked away by the sharp talons of an eagle, quite common in these parts. Maybe he had been shot or was lost forever in the endless woods. Distraught, I walked on for another hour until the dark consumed my search and then gave up, returning to the Little Red Cabin.

And there asleep by the back door was a curled-up bundle of vanilla-colored fur. It would not be the last time that Woody wandered away. But he taught me a golden rule to remember over many anxious separations in the years to come: *Woody the Dog always came back from where he left.*

Chapter 7

ZEN DOGGISM

Midsummer 1983

Up a short path from the back of the cabin stood a rickety outhouse. Above the door hung a crooked sign that read *King George the Turd*. My view from the throne looked down upon the ocean through feathery hemlocks. It was Midsummer Night, ten p.m., and the sun was still shining bright, high above the horizon. It wouldn't set until one in the morning.

Afterward, I went down to the edge of the reef and dangled my feet over the side. Woody sat next to me, peering into the water three feet down. We were sitting along Behm Canal on a shelf of ten-thousand-year-old black volcanic schist. It was formed in the Pleistocene, when glaciers receded and left behind the crumpled, scarred coastline of the Alexander Archipelago of which this island, Revillagigedo, was a part.

The reef, pocked full of holes, told stories with the sea. It slapped, gurgled, swished, and fizzed. To my left, it sang: *szzssssw, pbung, spulunk*. Below me, flushing in and out of a small grotto, came *buloogk . . . buloogk*. To the right, washing through a tiny inlet: *gerp, kunk, gerp*. And receding waves completed the orchestral arrangement with *ssSSaah . . . ssSSaah*—before returning to momentary stillness, then carrying on—a continuous, symphonic ebb and flow.

Chinook salmon were on their spawning run, and a three-foot fat one leapt and plopped into the sun-drunk sea. Large, slow rollers traversed the shore, wavelets rebounding and radiating in vibratory rings. Just below the surface, orange-yellow rockweed swayed in the current.

Woody appeared to be dreaming, just gazing at the play of light on water and following the path of the Alaska State Ferry on its way over to Prince of Wales Island. It all made me think of a poem by Li She:

> *All day I feel lost as if drunk or in a dream*
> *Then I hear spring is over and force myself*
> *   to climb*
> *Passing a bamboo courtyard I meet a*
> *   monk and talk*
> *And spend another afternoon beyond this*
> *   floating life.*

The Little Red Cabin was a one-room schoolhouse where I was studying solitude and awkwardly learning how to build fires, put gear oil in a chain saw, cook over a Coleman stove, cut away fallen trees, and do some clumsy carpentry.

Woody was learning basic vocabulary of walking together, sitting, and staying, which he picked up in an instant, plus more nuanced commands like shaking off outside and not to bark unless it was important. I began to wonder, though, who was teaching whom. He did not appear to be some being of lesser intelligence but one of surprising genius, a prodigy of intrinsic relationship to the earth.

Woody had a Taoist way of moving in the world that instructed me in a profound and timeless curriculum— about being in a body, in one's own bones, here, now. His principal lesson was simplicity. He had no schedule, woke up each day to discover what was happening in that instant, and moved forth with glad curiosity. The key, as far as I could tell, was that he stayed anchored in his senses, in the ever-present now.

He was the first creature I knew who didn't come pressed into a box. His body was built of interfitting, furry triangles: triangle ears, triangle head, triangle nose, the triangles of his legs when he walked, all arrayed along a horizontal cylinder. Woody was a magnificent rolling wave of spontaneous canine geometry.

He didn't expect right answers, approval, or anything different than what was happening. What would it be like for me to imagine the world as he might, as if it had no names, time, or descriptions? His dog bible had within it one commandment: *Go Outside*. When he heard that inner calling, which was often, he would wander over and lay his head along my leg, fix me in the eye, and begin a slow tail wag. He was practicing a kind of *Zen Doggism*: knowing that if he stared at an object long enough, it would eventfully move.

The weather never mattered. He did not care about the temperature, wind speed, or rains lashing against the cabin. There were times I didn't want to move from the relative warmth of our abode into a wet-sopped day. But in Southeast Alaska, if you let the rain dictate what you did, it was no place for you. So, begrudgingly, outfitted in rain gear and boots, I followed Woody out the door and into the deluge.

Once the downpour had its way, wetting my face with rivulets that seeped down my back, I learned to relax into the storm. The wind would flail the trees like a jet taking off, and then settle briefly before roaring down the runway again. The rain plopping on my raincoat, on the ground, on my face, made a wild percussive music as Woody moved through it all glad, embodied, fully alive.

Chapter 8

THE INTIMACY
OF LETTERS

Late Summer 1983

In the devotion to solitude, there sometimes arises a certain impulse to share a conversation, yet not to the point of wanting to abandon the vigil in wanton sociability. Chinese mountain hermits would revel in occasional visitors and a bottle of wine shared but, for the most part, maintained their seclusion. I really did want to be alone, and yet also felt an urge to connect with my fellow humans. Perhaps this is why we invented writing.

Nights in the cabin, my usual place was sitting at an old red Naugahyde recliner, a piece of plywood across its arms for my desk. By day, the beat-up picnic table on the porch served, with the ocean as my radio. Letter writing became my telephone to the world, my pass to a distinct kind of intimacy in solitude. Quiet discussions with friends occurred over many months, sharing images and experiences of life, one to another.

I wrote Whizz, a woman in Seattle I was infatuated with, wondering if she would come here. Not asking directly, just suggesting it—*be cool if you could see the place*—buddy-safe kind of language for fear of the answer. What a chicken! Not proud of it, but I was scared of girls, always had been, especially if attracted to them. Perhaps that was one reason I fled the city, to not have to face that.

Whizz wrote back in curly script, sometimes with stars at the tips of her *W*'s or the tail of her *R*'s. My older brother, Louie, wrote longhand in neat but fluid capital letters on lined engineering paper. Richard Buell, a poet friend, wrote postcards and letters banged out on his small Royal typewriter:

> *Wardo . . . the cruel joke of traffic jams, exhaust of 20th century drifting into blue sky of street. Horns honk down my throat. A Chevy flips me off. In general state of narrow-gauge paranoid city mind. Uptight lookaways and surface skating. I am here ??? sogged in surreal public tinsel, driving around in thick traffic in Volvo tank, mumbling mantras to keep sane . . . You in abandoned ashram by the sea, turning inward, staying at home.*
>
> *Single-heartedness is the wonder, and in that one spotlight, everything dances.*

The ritual of letter writing requires a slowing down and attention to many discrete steps. First, locate paper and pen— and write—then read it over imagining your friend reading it for the first time. Next, find an envelope and choose the stamp—appreciating the art of its miniature frame. Finally, address it and leave it in a box where a postman's hands will find and sort it. The letter will subsequently pass through four or five other pairs of hands to be delivered unexpectedly at its destination. Weeks later, a surprise response will appear waiting in your dark mailbox and the long-distance intimacy continues.

One thing about writing letters. It can get pretty old for a dog. It didn't seem fair for me to sit and write and Woody's only choice was to sleep. Here was a dilemma: to keep him inside with me, denying him his autonomous right to roam, his birthright to freedom, or let him go on his own. Woody was a full-hearted, open-eyed being, flowering in his unbound wonder of the world. I was exploring the grand drama of freedom in my life, how was it fair to deny him his? We lived in a remote place, so I took to leaving the porch door open. He could come and go as he pleased. The added benefit of the open door policy was wild sea air brushing the cabin clear.

Woody did like to wander and, to my dismay, occasionally for too long. My hunts for him would always end in failure, but hours later, inevitably, there came that single paw scratch at the back door. As he grew in size and energy, though, dog wanderings alone weren't doing the trick. He was of champion bloodline, a hunting dog of inexhaustible energy. It was like sharing the cabin with an Olympic athlete, always ready to go. I had to figure out a way to help him express his endless vigor while preserving mine.

One day, I started using a Frisbee for his dog dish. He'd shove it around the cabin with his feet to get my attention and, joyfully, would find it later filled with food. After a couple weeks of this, one day, he pushed it from one end of the cabin to the other, but I ignored him. He shoved it to my chair and looked up. I continued to write as if he weren't there. He flipped it up on edge with a paw, grabbed it between his canines, and dropped it on my lap. Then he took a step back and looked squarely at me, his tail slowly wagging. I tossed it a few feet away. He looked at it, looked at me, scraped it around the floor with his feet, and brought it back. Then I fed him. He started to understand this could be a game.

A week later on the beach, I let the Frisbee fly. Woody gazed up in wonder as his dog dish became this miraculous soaring thing that sailed over his head and far down the shore. Perhaps like me as a boy, looking up and seeing Apollo 11 moving across the Alabama heavens toward the moon, his dog universe suddenly expanded. He half ran, half jumped as he made his way to the Frisbee forty feet away.

Before long, Woody would romp after his dog dish as soon as I let it go and, like a kid trying to net a butterfly for the first time, make a clumsy attempt to grab it on the fly. He quickly matured his understanding of the game, though. One day, he raced down the beach, leapt, and bumped his nose against the Frisbee. When he landed, there it was, hanging from his lower canine tooth like a lip ring. He stood now, an initiate in the kingdom of Wham-O; a new era of dog life had begun.

As we walked back toward the red cabin, a flock of noisy mallards careened across the western sky over the ocean. Woody stared after them for some time. Then he turned and looked at me as if I had some part to play in this great mystery. Destiny beckoned to him from that horizon, and he didn't know why or what it was. Hundreds of years of genetic calling raced along his spine. Someday I'd need to answer that summons; I would need to fulfill the timeless equation between Woody and ducks.

He looked over his shoulder longingly at their disappearing shapes before following along.

Chapter 9

ACCOUNTING FOR TREES

Late August 1983

We jumped in the Rabbit to go see Cape Fox logging operations. As controller, I saw the money coming and going but had no idea what it meant on the ground. We drove north through Ketchikan and left the highway five miles out of town up Ward Cove Road through Forest Service land until entering Cape Fox property. Rounding a sharp turn on a logging road, a truck stacked with giant trees barreled straight for us. It couldn't or didn't try to slow down. I was barely able to slide our toy car to the edge and hung by a tread, teetering over a hundred-foot drop. The logging truck cleared us by inches.

We crossed a small bridge over a creek tumbling out of the hills and, farther up, reached a crew pioneering a road into virgin forest with dozers and dump trucks. Bouncing over the deeply rutted road in our Rabbit felt silly. The road guys, tough, weather-hardened men smoking cigarettes, eyed us with amusement.

The road building and logging company was a local, white-owned business contracted by Cape Fox. As part of the contract, they were required to hire some Native shareholders. A couple of new Cape Fox dump trucks filled with gravel went by. At the wheel of one of the trucks sat Willie Strong, Delores's youngest son. His hair was jet-black, crushed against his forehead, and his eyes smiled behind crooked glasses.

"Hey, what you white dogs doin' out here on Indian land?" he yelled at me.

"Just coming out to see how much you been sleeping on the job," I responded.

Willie laughed. "Not like you office guys. We're doin' all the hard work."

"Well, that's good," I said, tapping my temple. "Then my plan is working perfectly."

Willie waved and pulled the big truck away in a cloud of dust and roar. We parked the Rabbit in a turnout and began to climb a hill where I was told a logging crew would soon be working. We ascended through sword ferns, skunk cabbage, and devil's club until coming to a plateau at the bottom of a small waterfall. I lay back on the warm ground and suffered a quick face bath from Woody's tongue before he leapt away into the woods. The creek splashed across the rocks, and a raven *quorked* loud in the ancient trees. A green-and-blue dragonfly landed on my chest, its large, iridescent eyes peering at me, while a Pacific wren sang a mellifluous rhapsody answered up the valley by another. My hand ran over the rough scales of a nearby spruce that climbed into the sky forever.

By tomorrow, this little haven would be buried beneath a clear-cut.

I was sweating hard, climbing up a ridge through a forest of hemlock and spruce. Near the top, Woody was busy making friends with Cliff, a logger, who was sitting in the shade drinking from a thermos. Cliff was built like a barrel, in his early forties, with a ruddy complexion and long red sideburns. Mosquitoes swarmed around his head, but he ignored them as he ran his hands brusquely through Woody's coat.

"Good dog," he said, with a cigarette-scratched voice.

"Yeah, he's a keeper," I said. "Everything I need to know, I learned from him."

Cliff took off his hard hat to mop away the sweat from his forehead. He had a gash beneath his brow and a couple of wounds next to his nose.

"The boss punch you out?" I asked.

"These? Nah," he said, rubbing his crooked nose. "Dodged a widow-maker this morning. Came off a spruce I dropped." He waved it off. "Branch scratch, that's all."

"You get hurt much?"

"Nah." He laughed. "Broken collarbone, right forearm, busted-out knee, slipped disc, ruptured lung . . ." He looked off down the hill. Turning serious, he said, "I lost a good friend up here, a month ago."

The silence rose on the heat of the afternoon. A varied thrush called to its mate. Woody nosed around Cliff's lunch pail.

"Well, I ain't bein' paid gabbin' my jaw," he said, standing. "You want to see how it's done?"

I tied Woody to a tree uphill while Cliff filled his chain saw with gas and gear oil from plastic jugs. He fastened a thick belt holstered with metal wedges around his waist and approached a five-hundred-year-old spruce—a seedling when Columbus hit shore. Pacific wrens whistled, and a bee buzzed my ear. Cliff looked up at the tree for some time as if he were listening for a signal.

"Checking the wind," Cliff said. "Affects where it drops."

Cliff was the bullbuck of this logging side, the head feller. He was paid for the number of trees he brought down and kept a tally on a band inside his helmet. He could make up to $350 on a good day but wouldn't get paid a nickel for a busted tree. The two-hundred-foot spruce had to be brought down between two stumps with about three feet to spare.

Other saws buzzed along the hillside. Whistles from choker setters piped up. It was surreal to look down the valley, which was covered in old-growth trees, and realize that in a couple of days, a handful of men would reduce it to stumps. Cliff fired up his Husqvarna and bit into the butt of the tree. Six people could have linked arms around it. He went downhill to make the undercut. Every now and again, he stopped and looked to the top of the tree for any perceptible sway. He worked fast and climbed to the uphill side for the back cut. After slicing three feet in, he pulled the saw out and began to use the wedges from his belt, pounding them into the cut with a small sledgehammer. The air filled with the aroma of sapwood.

Woody watched all this intently. Cliff worked the tree for about twenty minutes, almost like a sculptor. He'd bang on the wedge and then look up to check the wind and the tree's fluctuation. He gave it three more sharp whacks, looked up one last time, and then began to hustle uphill toward me at a forty-five-degree angle away from it.

Nothing seemed to happen at first. Then, gradually, this goliath of the forest began to sway and slightly tilt. A series of small cracks sounded near the base. It started to list noticeably. When it reached thirty degrees, the tree snapped through to the undercut and began to fall in earnest. It ripped off adjacent tree limbs—widow-makers all—before crashing to the ground in a slow-motion, violent thrash. A reverberation from an object bigger than a dozen elephants rolled through the earth. A subterranean boom-fall echoed down the hillside announcing the tree's end.

Then everything grew preternaturally quiet. It had taken about a half hour to cut down a tree that had been growing in that spot for five centuries. Cliff had dropped it expertly between the two stumps with about a foot to spare on each side.

"Now that's what we call a pickle," he said. He walked along the trunk, delimbing it and getting it ready for the choker setter to wrap a cable around and drag it uphill to the spar. Cliff would knock ten more giants like this one to the ground before the day was done, then head to the Mecca Tavern for a night of drinking. As he looked up a hillside of stumps that had once been a forest, I asked him what he felt like after a day's work.

"Well," he said, and paused. A hush hung in the air. He looked away a bit, then shook it off. "It's a crop, you know. It'll grow back."

He walked on, lighting a cigarette—a tough man doing a tough job, with no time to consider such things.

We drove back to Saxman, and I began to wonder about it all, the paradox of a tribal culture that once lived on the land using minimal resources, now logging their lands like there was no tomorrow. The Cape Fox people clung to the sea in a small village of cedar clan houses, fronted by totem poles. A sophisticated, self-reliant people, they made wood dishes and bowls, halibut hooks, masks and canoes, cedar bark baskets, hats and robes. They had developed complex cultural systems, art, and theater, and harvested countless foodstuffs from the sea and forest. Their descendants had been bequeathed large swaths of virgin forest by Congress and, by necessity, had turned it over to white managers and logging companies who were, in turn, ripping the hillsides bare as fast as the Japanese would buy the trees.

Did the shareholders know what was really going on? A hidden distrust existed between the shareholder body and the corporation. I don't think anyone in the village really understood what we in the office did, especially me, an accountant who tracked gains and losses. It was a tense balance for me to walk. On one hand, I felt somewhat trusted in Saxman; at the same time, I sensed an underlying unease about me being non-Native and having a full-time job.

The Native board of directors were good folks, politically savvy, family people. But none had the requisite business experience to prepare them to oversee thousands of acres of forestland and tens of millions of dollars of assets and complex business enterprises, inside a rapidly created corporate structure that was foreign to them. The president of the company, the shareholders' representative on the management team, was a longshoreman. The chairman worked a swing shift at the LP sawmill. They were thrust into this situation; given millions of dollars and masses of land that were subject to local, state, and federal taxes and laws; and then expected to oversee it—all through the perplexing new lens of a for-profit corporation.

They had been set up for failure. Pressured by a shareholder body—mostly clamoring for quick financial distributions—the board put their trust in Dave Sisewell, who had little experience in the logging industry, a CEO with a twenty-thousand-acre playground of Tlingit-owned land. A man can make a lot of missteps with that before anyone notices.

We drove past Sisewell's sawmill. A new Komatsu log loader, a D6 Cat, and a fleet of shiny new pickups and crew cabs bought on credit were working the yard. The sawmill itself had cost more than $150,000 . . . so far. It was a hell of a tricky maneuver to build a sawmill in Alaska. There was a reason few such operations survived. But Dave was a dreamer. He was trying to do something good, to keep jobs at home and train Native shareholders to take them. But the risks were enormous, and everything was moving too fast.

All day long, I had seen one Native person directly benefiting from all this—a guy driving a truck. It left me with an empty feeling. The Tlingit people had been decimated by guns, diseases, racism, and economic privation. Two generations of welfare had left its mark, and alcohol had moved in to make sure the scars ran deep. But Alaska Natives were resilient and hardy people. Strong leaders had emerged who had kept their cultures alive.

Then along came the Alaska Native Claims Settlement Act, with its mindset of large industrial development. Rather than unity, the corporations were creating more division in a culture already deeply troubled. Thousands of acres of original forest were tumbling off the hillside from men just doing their jobs. I couldn't help feeling sick. The Tlingits were now on the front lines of our culture's way of fragmenting and destroying ecosystems.

Just trust us, we said. You'll make a lot of money.

Chapter 10

DOG HOCKEY

September 1983

Woody trundled down the sloshy path ahead of me in the rain as I wrestled two five-gallon jerry jugs into the kitchen. We had driven five miles down the road to a community fill-up, which consisted of a hose poking out of a forested creek on the side of the highway.

I hung up my rain gear and sat down on a wood stool just inside the door to take off my *Ketchikan sneakers*, the calf-length XTRATUF boots that everyone here wore. The problems of Saxman stood a world away from the red cabin. Here, a new struggle was underfoot; fall season was imminent, bringing with it chill and darkness. Today featured the twelfth day of continuous rain. It would be followed by two hundred more—six times' Seattle's rainfall. The days began to feel like a coffin lid slowly closing.

Rain beat down on the cabin roof like nails. I fell into writing a love letter to Whizz while quickly working my way through a bottle of Beaujolais. The sky had dropped so far that only the porch rail was visible before a seamless wall of gray. Green firewood smoldered in the stone fireplace. Naively, I had put off cutting my winter's supply, a mistake that would haunt me in the months to come.

The tide was low, and the ocean chuckled and gurgled against the sea wall. Buoyed by the confidence of rushing wine, I wrote.

> *Dear Whizz,*
>
> *It's raining, the clouds are low, impenetrable, while the lighthouse, a pendulum of time, whirls about in calm silence, anchoring the coming darkness. I find in the lighthouse a comfort. It keeps count always there, a heartbeat . . . reminding me that all was here before me and will be thereafter.*
>
> *I was taken by surprise by the sudden encroachment of fall . . . a rookie move. In a remote cabin, not knowing that spring is the season to cut firewood, instead of late August . . . Ha! Which is to say, the meager fire sputtering away in the fireplace is not a recipe for coziness and I wear a lot of sweaters indoors. Yet Woody is here in his ever-present acceptance and curiosity, and nature enwraps us always.*
>
> *What am I doing . . . ? Someday I will beat in time to the waves, the rain, the wind through the trees, and the seagulls flying patterns through the turbid sky. I guess I'm choosing to be alone to hear what the raw world wants to say to me or what Woody wants to say to me. I'm listening.*

I hesitated and took a few more slugs of wine from the bottle, which was growing perilously low . . .

> *Dr. Woody is telling me to write you . . . I think of you, effervescent tiny bubbles in your wake, handing out coffee and giving hope to the walking dead with your own beaming lighthouse of goodwill. Glittering deep, bright eyes, laughing smile, dancing swirl . . .*

The pen hung over the paper for a long time. Another couple draughts from the bottle emptied it. Working toward inviting Whizz to visit, I chickened out. More wine was needed.

I pulled on the XTRATUFs and was out the door with Woody to make a run to the Lighthouse Grocery three miles down the highway. The woods were dark, and the rain beat steady on my rubber coat. I was able to navigate the crooked path without a light by something I called *foot seeing*. Trees are darker than the night sky. So by looking up rather than down when you walk in the forest, you can often discern the path beneath your feet by following the dim trail in the sky.

The wine, of course, made trusting a walk in the dark easier. At the top of the ramp, Woody hopped aboard the tailgate on our new ride: a rusted-up $150 Chevy pickup. As we barreled up the gravel road, the distinctive engine pings inspired the barking of a hidden dog. Woody anticipated the upcoming combat. He got ready in the bed of the pickup, peering forward into the rain for first sight of the Norwegian elkhound with a very bad temper. When we had first moved into the Little Red Cabin, the elkhound had taken a strong dislike to Woody, who returned the favor.

Woody girded up, his tail waving stalwartly for the feral joust ahead. As we rounded the last corner to the elkhound's house, he eagerly stood up on the rear wheel well. The other dog's barks rose in high-pitched shrillness. Woody steeled his eyes.

Here he came . . . busting out of the brush, possessed, yapping jaws at Woody, who flared his teeth, the hair on the back of his neck raised. The elkhound ran alongside the truck and jumped, trying to nab a piece of Woody's flesh. It was foolish, really. Woody had an uphill advantage and snapped down at the hound while letting out a primal snarl that would have scared a big hunter on a campfire night. The elkhound followed us for about a hundred feet before falling away and disappearing behind trees. Woody's tail wagged triumphantly, eyes drunk with victory.

We reached the top of the hill as the sky succumbed to total darkness. As we turned south and chugged down the highway, the rain doubled in strength and hammered on the truck like a kettledrum. Woody moved forward, crouching against the back window for protection, as I—more wine affected than first thought—struggled to keep the truck on the pitch-black road.

There was a second problem. The headlights on the Chevy started to dim, and the windshield wipers slowed. The alternator had failed, and the battery was dying fast. A mile from the store, I prayed we'd make it in time. We just did, clattering into the gravel parking lot as the headlights faded to an amber glow that wouldn't have attracted a moth. I shut the engine down and coasted to the front door to reserve what battery was left. How the hell were we going to get back?

Inside, I picked up two bottles of wine and a Big Dad Beef Stick for Woody. Then a spark of an idea hit me. I added two disposable flashlights and, with some rusty wire from the pickup bed, rigged up a flashlight to each headlight. Woody, sopping wet, jumped up front with me. There was just enough juice to turn the motor over once until it caught, and I pulled up to the edge of the gravel lot.

The road in both directions was as black as a river of tar, disappearing into the night sky. A car passed by, and I gunned it, a bit excited about my crafty experiment. The flashlights were working! Trouble was, they only worked up to five miles an hour; above that, they were useless, completely obliterated by the rain and the night. The windshield wipers dragged to a stop. I had to lean my head out the window pummeled by the rain to see ahead.

Sixty feet down the road from the store, we had to stop. The truck was consumed in darkness. I couldn't even see my hands on the steering wheel. Worse, there was no shoulder on the road, only ditches. The only way out was to back down the highway to the parking lot. Just then, in my rearview mirror, a pair of headlights rounded the curve a quarter mile back, coming at us at forty miles an hour. We couldn't make the parking lot in time, and with no taillights, we were sitting ducks.

Desperate, I looked forward. Fifty yards up, a car was just about to disappear around a corner. If I could keep his taillights in sight, we might make it. Flooring it and moving through the three gears as fast as possible, my head out the window, going forty-five, eyes stinging from the rain, I had to imagine the arc of the highway ahead by tracing the curve of the disappearing red taillights in front.

Meanwhile, with the headlights behind us closing in, we were committed, nothing to do but keep it floored for two miles while the road twisted left and right back to the South Point Higgins Road. I would have laughed if not scared to death.

But Providence rode with us that night. We barreled off the highway to Point Higgins just as the car behind zipped by. We coasted down the hill, me looking up at the sky path in the trees to tell where the road was. Though silent, we did not slip by unnoticed. The elkhound made his run at the truck. Woody extended his body halfway out the window, his tail spinning like helicopter blades, baring his teeth, snarling and snapping at his black-nosed enemy, telling the devil himself to get back in the grave.

We pulled into the clearing and stumbled down the path to the cabin. Back inside, a small flame from the embers of the fire and the Beaujolais warmed my insides enough to finish the letter to Whizz. Inspired to tell her about our store run, I wrote madly. But the more I imagined her with me, the more it appeared a fantasy. Whizz was a city girl, an opera singer, cultured in fine art. What would she be doing in a cold cabin with a guy and his dog on the edge of the ocean? The wine, though, infused me with a crazy hope and kept me writing, but the words grew clumsier.

Woody began clowning around with a sock and doing what he could to entertain himself. The rain beat against the cabin, and I wadded up the letter to Whizz and threw it against the window, frustrated by the folly of the whole affair. A moment later, the paper returned to my lap. Woody was standing back with his eyes aflame. I tossed the paper again. He rushed after it and brought it back and spit it out on my lap. A dozen times, Woody raced to grab it.

It was then, on a rain-hurled night in a remote cabin in Southeast Alaska, that we invented *dog hockey*. A wadded-up newspaper wrapped in duct tape became the puck. A step leading into the kitchen served as one goal, the other an open door into a back room. Woody was the goalie. I started at one end of the cabin and began to skate toward him in my socks. He stood up and ran at me. I took a shot, but quick as a rabbit, Woody closed his legs, deflected the puck, and nabbed it with his mouth. He ran around the cabin in a victory lap, then dropped it in front of me and backed up, step by step, until he was in the goalie position again, his head low, waiting for the next rush on the goal.

I skated toward him. He rose up. Faking left, I dodged right and shot. The puck snapped through his legs and banged into the refrigerator. *Goall!* I yelled. *Goallllllll!* Woody ran to get the puck, came back, dropped it at my feet, and backed up for the next run.

From the shore through our curtainless window, a passerby would have seen a wine-filled man and a yellow dog tirelessly engaged in a fierce all-night battle of dog hockey, yelling and running around in total joy as the lighthouse spun its charm through the dark.

Chapter 11

FAMILY

October 1983

In the frosty dawn, a pair of mallards careened around the river bend like flying bowling pins. I rose from stiffened knees, brought the shotgun to shoulder height, pointed it vaguely in the direction of the quacking pins, and blasted. The boom shocked the morning air, hit the mountain across the river, and bounced back threefold in strength. Woody popped up and jumped halfway into the water, looking expectantly for the splash—his signal to do what thousands of years of genetic programming had wired him to do—to leap into the bracing river, feet pumping and tail navigating, straight for the feathered prize.

There was no splash. The ducks swept out of the picture like phantoms. Woody stood up to his knees amid the river grasses, looking after the disappearing ducks as if a curtain had come down prematurely on a good movie. He turned to me. *What???? I've been hovering in the cold with you for an*

hour and a half? And this . . . ? He just stood there, this powerful, capable, young hunting dog, looking right at me. I was
six foot, two inches of abashed man, ashamed by a Labrador
cheated of his birthright.

Come on, man. Vamos, I said. After leaving our duck hide-
out and climbing up the little rise to the logging road, I turned
back. Woody hadn't moved. He was still planted in the river up
to his knees, just staring at me.

Back at the cabin, a letter from my brother Louie informed me
he had gotten himself a golden retriever and wanted to come
up for a fall duck hunt with our two young dogs to a remote
lake on Prince of Wales Island. He proceeded to specify the
exact shotgun for me to buy and neatly listed out a five-day
menu for us on index cards. Engineer Louie didn't make any
move that was not exhaustively planned. I dashed him a quick
wine-drunk postcard, telling him to bring on the mergansers.

I never fancied myself a hunter, but the stirring inside
Woody—the generations of British Isles calling, the ancestors
shivering on the foggy flats in the duck blinds, the feathered
prize brought proudly back to praising hands—had inspired
me for his sake to try.

Louie shipped me up a Remington 870 pump-action shotgun, initiating my practice at the local rod and gun club, hitting two out of ten skeet on a good day. I took a liking to guns
and also picked up a used .357 Magnum at a garage sale.

Figuring it was time for Woody to be introduced to his first
gunshot, we drove to the end of the road and trekked across
the squishy muskeg. Forty yards from a cedar snag, I raised my
index finger—the signal for him to sit. Woody lowered his rear
end slowly and stared intently at me with impeccable focus,
sensing something of import in the air.

The .357 slipped easily from its worn leather holster. I
raised the blue-black barrel toward the snag. Woody sat still

as a statue. Taking aim and slowly squeezing the trigger, the blast made my ears ring and echoed off the steep mountain above. As acrid blue smoke wafted in the air, I turned to see how Woody had taken his first shot. A vanilla-colored blur streaked by me. He was gone, full-tilt boogie down the clearing following the scent of the bullet, hopping over bush and branch, leaping through the muskeg to uncover the wild mystery. He tracked the spent bullet trail to the gray snag and circled it, his tail wagging like a sail in a taut wind, nose to earth searching for something. Gunplay was in his DNA.

Back home, via a device I had seen in a hunting magazine, Woody's training involved retrieving a hard white cylinder, propelled a hundred feet out to sea by a .22 blank. He would sit on the beach, shivering with excitement, and after the blast, gaze in complete amazement as the cylinder ascended into the sky and fell into the ocean like an Apollo capsule.

When I whispered, *Woody*, he'd take off, the great leap of ages, breast crashing through waves and swimming to the floating capsule. He'd snatch it out of the water, whip his head around, and paddle back to shore, snorting through his nostrils. Finally, he would drop the cylinder at my feet and slowly back up the beach, looking like a dripping white wolf, ready for the next blastoff.

Louie; his wife, Franny; and golden retriever, Jake, were arriving on Alaska flight 67 at the airport on Gravina Island, across from Ketchikan. I decided to pick them up in the twenty-one-foot Sabrecraft I had bought from my dad. The boat had appeared in numerous recurrent dreams of mine over the years, always floating away from the dock. Sometimes I'd run after it, sometimes my dad would be in it. Almost compulsively, I bought that same boat in the waking world. Was it some attempt to connect with him by possessing his cast-off vessel?

The twelve nautical miles to the airport were as rough as my relationship with him—clear but blustery, with twenty-five-knot winds from the north and five-foot seas. Woody tried his best to stay upright, finally hunkering down up front.

At the airport dock, the crew came aboard. Jake and Woody became instant rivals and friends. The five of us pounded across to Ketchikan to one of Woody's favorite hangouts, the Arctic Bar. The Arctic was a roughed-up, one-story joint on the main drag, built on pilings over the water. Its logo was of two bears humping. You found the Arctic just north of a short tunnel blasted through a cliff that separated Ketchikan into two. Across the street, long wooden stairs ascended a steep rock wall to houses on the hillside.

Woody bopped out back to the deck and greeted his friends, any drunks who might engage in a little game of retrieve the beer cap or make an offering of a cocktail pepperoni stick. The deck of the Arctic was a special place where crunched-faced Alaskans, ruddy-cheeked skiff girls, cannery workers, artists, fishermen, and the adrift all sat in fall afternoon glinting sun watching the fishing boats, having a smoke, and gazing at the crisp outline of trees and crooked homes on Pennock Island. It was an idyllic place to get loaded on long summer days and nights and a spot to lose your mind in the middle of winter after three months of rain.

We ordered beers on the deck until the setting sun drove us reluctantly out to the Sabrecraft for the wild-ass, hour-long ride north. By the time we docked again, both dogs were seasick.

Franny, Louie, and Jake were my first visitors to the Little Red Cabin. Louie was my best friend in the family, the only one who somewhat understood my exodus to Alaska and the need to get away from the force field of my upbringing. While he admired my quest for freedom, his path had taken a more structural turn. Louie was earthbound, a solidly built engineering prodigy who faced life within a strict code of ana-lytics. He was the handiest guy I ever met. Louie could invent, fix, or design his way out of anything. Inanimate things spoke to him and told him what they needed. He had followed our dad's footsteps and worked at Boeing, becoming a liaison engineer whose daily job was to fix any glitches that came off the flight line with any plane. Louie never met a mechanical problem that failed him.

He understood the hidden architecture of material things; he could walk into a room and discern the pressure loads on walls; he could tell you why a particular boat hull created the least drag in the water. Louie discoursed on night-sky radiation or could tell you why an airliner was engineered around its landing gear. He also brewed the best beer in the world and shipped it up to me in a specially designed box that held twelve bottles, that he labeled as *BOOKS* on the outside. The lady at the post office remarked to me once, "You sure read a lot."

As a teenager, Louie had been the first to dare to dissent within our strict, authoritarian family. He grew his hair long, did drugs, and had a special talent for evoking deep enmity from the principal of the high school. While I became the family clown, and busied myself making sure I pleased teachers and was liked by everyone around me, Louie drifted into dope, small crime, fast cars, and troublemaking. He introduced twelve-year-old me to an underground world of heavy metal and psychedelic music and demonstrated a way of life outside the lines I was too timid to emulate. But since his wilder days, Louie had discovered his higher calling as an engineer and straightened out his life path.

That night, at the Little Red Cabin, we laid out our provisions. Franny set to work in the kitchen making food for the hunting trip. A former high school cheerleader, of medium height, with a work-forged slim frame and blue eyes, Franny was an anachronism. She should have been a pioneer in the

Old West. She didn't belong with high-rise buildings, sleek cars, and supermarkets. Franny was a countrywoman, impeccable and compulsive about order and cleanliness. She was doing her best in a bare cabin, the abode of a big dog and a man with questionable housekeeping skills. She was also four months pregnant with her first child.

"You know, Ward," she said as she hefted a five-gallon jerry jug of water up over her burgeoning baby belly and onto the counter. "If you ever want a woman in your life . . . you're going to have to get running water." She blew the hair from her eyes and poured the jug into the sink to clean the dishes.

Jake was busy eating Woody's chow. A healthy and hyperactive golden retriever, Jake was a tad insecure, especially around Woody. Every time Woody went near his bowl, Jake would shove him out of the way and gobble up as much as he could. Woody accepted the impudence of his first-ever visitor with a kind tolerance, a Taoist gracefulness of being the guest in one's own home. He allowed himself to be pushed out of the way without surrendering a hair of his innate nobility. To see a dog with an almost spiritual level of forbearance was humbling.

Louie had the shotguns out on the bare wood floor, cleaning them, quiet as usual, his six-foot durable frame and dark brows concentrating on the task. Jake and Woody began wrestling, tumbling over, clashing teeth, crashing into chairs, then boxing, incisors flashing, growling. Woody chewed on Jake's face and got boxed back hard. I looked around the fire-lit cabin, everyone engaged in some focused task, and felt for the first time in my life a true feeling of belonging, of family.

Chapter 12

TRUCKA DE LA DUCKA

October 1983

The next morning dawned bone-stiff cold. I had slept on the floor of the small side room shivering in my sleeping bag. In the main room, the frosty exhalations of Franny, Louie, and two dogs had fogged over the window. Franny cleared a spot to watch a large eagle on the beach, its white head gleaming. I made coffee while Louie stoked the fireplace—which he did not approve of at all, schooling me on "the superior heat-exchange efficiency" of a woodstove. We stood looking out the window as the coffee warmed our hands and insides. Sapphire-blue waves crested with snowy tops were wind-blown into sunlight.

Then the ocean exploded.

Two killer whales shot out of the water like submarine missiles and crashed back in slow-motion majesty, rolling huge waves over the reef. We yelled and whooped. Woody and Jake jumped up, and we all tore out of the cabin and down to the beach. A large pod cruised along the reef—fifteen giants, their ebony flukes glistening. The dogs ran in circles like madmen. We hustled along the shore, our little shouts swallowed by the great percussive blasts of blowholes misting in the air. When we ran out of beach, we watched the wolves of the sea move on, their glistening bodies disappearing down the coast.

We took this as a momentous sign of good fortune and spent the morning expectantly packing. Our destination was a Forest Service cabin at a remote lake on Prince of Wales Island. By noon, everything was loaded into the rusted-up Chevy. I had built a ramshackle flat roof out of wood to cover the dogs and our gear in the truck bed. Louie hung a little plywood sign on the back: *Trucka de la Ducka.*

I took the wheel, Louie rode shotgun, with Franny between us.

"How's the spare tire?" Louie asked.

"Fine. Don't worry about it," I said. I hadn't had a flat in years.

We took the small ferry over to Prince of Wales and drove up island as the afternoon light faded. A misty rain began to fall, and Woody and Jake were happy to have their little roof over them, noses filled with the beguiling odors of forest, wolf, chain-saw gas, tar, and lupine.

The drive was longer than we figured, and by the time we got to Sweetwater Lake, dark had descended. We hiked down to the shore and prodded around with our flashlights. No cabin. We did, though, find a small skiff pulled up against the rocky beach. There was a gunshot hole in the bottom, but it didn't seem to be letting in too much water. We decided to search for the cabin by boat. I used a little cedar cone to plug the gunshot hole, and we loaded in our gear and dogs and four-month pregnant mom. Louie cranked up the Johnson 15. The lake was beginning to freeze over, and we had to crunch through thin ice. Woody and Jake leaned forward on either side of me as my flashlight poked into the dark.

The lake was still in an unsettling way. Tortured and twisted trees along the shoreline seemed to reach out for us. The sound of the Johnson echoing from the woods announced our presence to all the hidden world. Expecting to see slavering red eyes in the forest caught by my flashlight's beam, I was glad to be flanked by 160 pounds of raw dog energy.

Then, straight out of a horror movie set, the cabin appeared, small and shadowy brown, engulfed by black trees. Louie aimed toward the beach and cut the engine. The aluminum hull crunched the sand and small waves lapped ashore. We stepped out, walked up the little porch, and opened the cabin door.

Inside, our flashlights revealed not an empty cabin but a bare room filled with guns, playing cards, sleeping bags, a half-opened Campbell's soup can, and dirty clothes. A Bowie knife, shotgun shells, and Rainier beer cans were strewn on a wood table. The air smelled of burnt beans, men, and oil.

No one spoke. We expected the beams of our flashlights to pass across a bloody body. If we felt spooked before, it was downright creepy now. We suddenly jumped at a distant sound—men's angry voices yelling, like a hive of stirred-up bees. We went outside and saw flashlights waving down the shore where we had picked up the boat.

"Hey, goddammit, bring that boat back!"

"Goddammit. Hey!"

"*Shit!* Goddammit!"

We climbed into the skiff and made our way slowly back along the path through the ice. The men continued to yell. As we got closer, their flashlights cut across us like lightsabers. We could make out the outlines of four men toting guns. Just a couple weeks before, two people had been killed at a nearby lake during a shootout at a Forest Service cabin over an argument. It felt like any moment a shot would ring out and a bullet would rip through my chest. I put my arm around Woody, realizing that I'd take the bullet for him if need be.

"Hey!" I yelled. "We got a pregnant lady here."

"What the hell you taking the boat for?" sputtered a guy in a camo hunting jacket, chewing tobacco and rocking his 30.06 in small circles. Another guy, stoutly built, with a scratchy little mustache and wearing an LP cap, seemed itching for a fight.

"Hey," Louie said to them with a fatherly inflection as the boat crushed against the sand. "If you can settle down a moment, we'll explain. I don't think we pose any threat to you gentlemen."

Woody hopped out and went over to the biggest guy of the bunch, tire-bellied and black-bearded. He couldn't help but reach down and pet him. Somehow this simple gesture took the edge off the situation. The guy calmed his friends down.

Louie explained the situation to them. I told them we had the cabin reserved for the weekend. This set up a howl of protest from the guy in the pulp mill cap.

"No way! We got it tonight. We got it reserved," he said. His little mustache flicked over lips as taut as piano wires. Stupidly, I had left the receipt for the cabin rental back in Ketchikan. These guys were lying, but I couldn't prove it. We negotiated a settlement. They would spend the night in the cabin, and we would camp out on the beach. Tomorrow the place would be ours.

It was a cold sleeping-bag night, the clear sky brimming with stars. Pulling Woody inside with me helped some. It ain't easy sharing a sleeping bag with a seventy-pound dog. He shivered through the night, maybe dreaming of ducks and leaping whales.

Early the next morning, a big raven woke us up to tell stories. We heard the outboard coming across the lake. When it hit shore, the tough guys were quiet, almost sheepish. Maybe they felt a little bad for making a pregnant woman sleep on a frozen beach. But they didn't apologize and left quickly.

We motored over to the cabin, swept it out, and moved in. Later, Louie and I cracked through the ice with the boat, and Louie even shot a duck that Woody plunged in and retrieved. Back in the boat, he shook and spiral-danced around, drenching us in celebration of the first duck feathers in mouth. Life force pulsed through his body and eyes, his birthright fulfilled—at least for now. Jake grabbed the bird from Woody's mouth and proudly held it up for Louie as if he had done the work.

We cooked up the merganser that night on a campfire. It tasted like spoiled fish, so we fed it to the delighted dogs. Franny, Louie, and I sang songs and joked and got drunk on boxed wine as a billion stars showered their grace upon us.

The next morning, by the time I got out of the bunk, the woodstove was going. Franny had made breakfast, and Louie was outside with a small bag of tools, working on the outboard. Woody and Jake were gnawing on each other's faces. I fed them some dog food. Jake finished his, then went after Woody's.

"With luck," I told them, "you'll both be eating duck again tonight." Making my way onto the porch with a steaming cup of coffee, I said to Louie, "Hey, man."

"Wassy!" he said playfully, calling me by my childhood nickname, derived from my initials, WAS.

I wandered down to the shore. "What's the problem?" Outfitted in Carhartt suspenders, Louie had the cowl of the engine up and was assessing the lower spark plug in the dim morning light.

"This plug is wet," he said. "The insulation on the wire is cracked."

"Meaning?" I asked. Not born with the engineering gene, yet handy in an offbeat way, I could usually get myself out of a scrape, but more with tape and wire and boards that didn't quite fit right. My dad; oldest brother, Jim; and Louie could fix almost anything. Of them all, however, Louie's mechanical prowess reigned supreme.

"It means the plug wire is shorting against the plate that holds the magneto," he said. "That's why it isn't firing."

"Are we screwed?"

"No, I can tie the plug wire back so that it doesn't arc on the magneto plate," he explained. "Or I could cut the wire off where the crack occurred and move the plug wire connector to the new location. It's got enough length to do that."

He fished in his overalls for a pocketknife. Hands oblivious to the cold, he pulled the cap off the wire, cut and trimmed back the insulation, wired it down, and screwed the plug back in. He gave the starter rope three pulls, and the outboard fired up, good as new.

We grabbed shotguns, lunch, and dogs and pushed off, breaking through the thin ice across the water's shell-pink face. The boat putted toward a small inlet at the end of Sweetwater Lake leading to Barnes Lake. Migratory birds, ducks, and geese used the inlet as a flyway heading toward breeding grounds down south. Woody and Jake sat in front with me, peering with unbridled delight into the frozen air. Every now and then, Woody rapturously ran his nose along the barrel of the shotgun.

We slowed near the inlet to Barnes and waited. Louie sipped on a thermos of coffee. The dogs rolled into shivering balls on the bottom of the boat, lulled to sleep by wave pings on the aluminum hull. A flight of ducks wheeled down the inlet, but we were too slow on the uptick and didn't even get the guns in the air.

"They fly like fucking missiles," I said.

Louie steered the boat a bit farther offshore so we would have more warning for the next flock.

"So what would you say are the guiding principles on your life journey?" Louie asked. He often posed philosophical questions to me as a prelude to proposing an insight into my way of life. He admired my quest for freedom, but often with a subtext that I might feel more successful if better grounded in life's physical practicalities.

While considering my answer, I heard a sound that reached inside and stopped me short. Woody looked up. Passing high above in the blue morning canopy was a V of snow geese, their throated saxophone honks echoing from hillside to hillside. They circled the lake, looking for a place to land.

We motored toward them and cut the engine—it was illegal to be in a boat under power while hunting. Just as we slowed, the geese rose and circled to the far end of the lake. And so the morning went, we sneaking toward them and they flying away and settling back down in the place we had just left.

"I guess one of my operating principles," I said, "is to maximize my freedom within the system."

Louie took another sip of coffee. "How's that working out for you?" He was an ally, but my refusal to work my way up through the system perplexed him. It was contrary to his path, his father's and grandfather's before him. To get away from the family to "find myself" seemed to him a vague and illusory campaign.

"I just don't want to dance to anyone else's tune no more, man," I said. "The system is fractured and so am I. Nature's getting pummeled and commerce is God."

Louie looked away. The faraway geese rested peacefully. Woody unfolded his neck and laid it over Jake's back and closed his eyes again.

"I guess I'm just trying to figure out how to do it my way," I added.

"Hmm," Louie said. He sucked down more coffee from his thermos cup. "Well, when you live by your own rules without compromise, be careful you don't wind up alone at the end of the world." He cranked up the motor.

I laughed again, but with a hollow tone. Louie's words flushed up a hidden dread from the bush. While dedicated to my newfound solitude, the idea of missing out on a woman or a family of my own haunted me.

We angled our way across the lake toward where the geese seemed to be heading. They settled down, but then flew away as we approached. Only half-heartedly did I want to shoot anything and prayed the geese would stay out of our range. I was a lousy hunter.

The first time I killed a bird, a lovely orange-breasted robin, I was eight years old. In Alabama, our yard was just across from Monte Sano Mountain in Huntsville and full of maples and pines and dogwoods. My best friend was Steve Sims, and his dad was a former marine drill instructor who scared me to death. Mr. Sims would sometimes have Steve or his brothers bent over holding their ankles in the front yard and whip them with his belt for the entire neighborhood to see. Physical punishment was the lay of the land then, with my share courtesy of dad's blistering hand and rarely understanding why. "Because I'm your father; that's why," is all he ever said.

Steve and his brother, Thumper, had BB guns, which prompted me to petition Dad for my own. On Christmas, there it was, a shiny new 1965 Daisy Western pump. It looked like the one Chuck Connors used on *The Rifleman*. I ran over to the Simses' place, and we started a regular series of war games in the woods. We'd hide behind logs and shoot at each other's barely visible heads as we popped up to shoot back. Amazing that one of us didn't lose an eye. If our parents had known about it, we'd all have gotten whipped.

When alone, shooting at trees was my game—or cans on the ground, or plastic army men in sand piles. Then I noticed a more challenging target—the birds that hopped and dove and hid among the branches of the trees in our yard. Long into the day until it was too dark to see, the Coke-bottle-eyed hunter stalked them. For weeks, he stayed on the quest. Lucky for them, he was a crummy shot.

Until one day, a young robin sat unwittingly on a branch unaware of the great hunter below. Leaning against a tree, taking aim down the sight, with my face against the plastic handle, I squinted and fired. The BB whisked away. To my absolute surprise and wonder, the robin dropped off the branch like a pine cone onto the grass. I rushed over and picked up my prize and ran my fingers through its orange chest feathers to its warm body underneath. Its eyes were closed as if it were simply asleep. And then in a moment of stupendous awakening for a little boy, I realized the bird would never open its eyes again and I was the cause of it—never before putting together the act of shooting with the reality of its effect.

My Daisy rifle hit the ground, tears blurred my eyes, and snot ran out of my nose. I went in and got my dad to show him my crime. He put his hand on my back and took me inside to find a shoebox. Then he got a shovel and let me pick a place in the front yard where he dug a tiny grave and had me bury the only bird I swore I'd ever kill. Down in my dad's shop, I cut and pounded together a small cross and drove it into the ground at the head of the robin's grave.

Back at Sweetwater, the geese flew along the shoreline in a long arc from east to south. Louie put us on a course to intersect them. This time, they did not turn away but kept coming. Louie shut down the engine. The dogs sat at attention, and we loaded our guns with ammo. Louie had brought a few shells along with larger shot in them, designed to bring down bigger birds.

The flock of twelve birds kept coming, oblivious to the danger that lurked in the dark boat below. Their calls radiated over the tree-circled lake like Gregorian chants in a cathedral—a beautiful flying troupe in October cold air—luminous, white-honking angels. They seemed to sing for the astonishing pleasure of being free and flew so close I could see their eyes looking back.

Louie lifted up the Remington and blasted . . .

The world tripped into slow motion. One of the geese gagged, faltered, and fell from her flock of companions. She descended in a grotesque crash into the mirrored lake. The flock carried on except for the fallen one's mate, who turned back and, stunned by the grief of it, circled his wounded lover with deep-belly plaintive calls.

The doomed bird floated upright with calm, accepting grace. She made soft pleas to her companion as if to say, Go . . . Go on, my love . . . Goodbye . . . We can never part.

The entire morning, putting around in the little boat with dogs and brother, I was content to not kill anything, secretly hoping we'd fail. Horrified at the scene before us, my heart numbed. Perhaps witnessing the enormity of the pain was too much, and I wanted it over. Or with a twisted sort of logic, I knew that it was important to not let myself off the hook, rationalizing it as something that Louie did; I was equally complicit in the agony we had unleashed into the world. Whatever the reason, I watched myself level the gun at the injured bird and pull the trigger. A boom bounced off the surrounding hills. The goose's head, brimmed in elegance, simply dipped beneath the water as if looking for lake grass. It floated with grand, impeccable grace, even more beautiful in death than I thought possible. And then the anguished call of its mate echoed over the lake as it flew away, a sound that knifed into my soul.

Louie sprang into action and had Jake jump out of the boat, who swam back snorting with a bird almost as large as he was.

I lifted its downy-feathered body into the boat as Louie hoisted in Jake, who showered us with water and excitement.

"All right, man!" Louie exclaimed.

Looking at the bird's lifeless slit of an eye took away my tongue. Louie fired up the engine, and we made our way across the cold lake. I wondered if, like the Ancient Mariner, I had just brought doom upon myself by killing the bird. The two geese had a lifelong bond of love, and we had shattered it.

As we hit the beach, I steadied myself with the practiced rationality that hunters, soldiers, farmers, cops, and murderers use when they have killed, a calcifying of the heart that justifies the taking of another's life. Woody and Jake bounded joyfully from the boat. Louie and I unloaded our gear and brought the dead bird up to the porch.

We set up a camera and took a time exposure of us holding the bird by its wing tips on the porch, with Jake and Woody below. We wore our hunting caps and long, rubber-booted overalls. I stared at the camera as a man who had done a tough and necessary thing, my large mustache crooked, my eyes straight and level. Woody tipped his head back, his nose luxuriating deep into the bird's feathers.

That night, I drank more than my share of boxed wine, then lay awake all night, haunted by the surviving goose's anguished lament.

Chapter 13

THE ABYSS

October 1983

The next morning, bleary with grief, I half-heartedly helped pack up. I was no hunter, why pretend? Thick ice made a boat exit impossible, so hiking out was our only option. We walked a mile along a small creek, beneath cedars and spiky spruces, avoiding the devil's club when possible. We came out on the road a quarter of a mile from Trucka de la Ducka, loaded up, put the dogs in the back, and headed down the highway.

A cold rain began to fall. Woody and Jake huddled together in their little condominium, dipping their noses into folds of fur. Louie was driving. *Bumpa-bumpa-bump.* Flat tire.

We changed the tire and drove on.

"We better not get another one," Louie said.

Just before sunset, we pulled into Craig, a sorry little fishing and logging town on the west coast of Prince of Wales, surrounded by clear-cuts. We checked into a crummy one-story hotel on the edge of downtown. The next morning, we would make the two-hour drive to catch the Hollis ferry back to Ketchikan.

I needed a drink. We put Jake and Woody in the front of the truck and walked up the street toward the Craig Inn Bar, a two-story, storm-washed pink building from the early 1900s. A humpback-whale skull with a set of deer antlers above it presided over the front door. Inside, our nostrils were assailed by the aroma of a thousand fights, blood and beer ground into the floor, then swashed out with an old mop. We picked a table on the side, and Louie went up and got some beers.

Out the window, the door of a gray day was closing fast, and a gloom enveloped the harbor. Seiners turned on their thousand-watt lamps, as bright as a Hollywood set. Just then, a shadow rose over our table. We looked up to find an enormous man-wall standing there, a three-hundred-pound sack of black beans looking directly down at Franny. Our conversation dwindled beneath his gaze. Maybe he was the guy who had killed the humpback over the door.

His head was the size of a large and spoiled pumpkin, surrounded by matted hair so thick it seemed pulled from the darkest fibers of the earth. We couldn't see his lips beneath his beard, just a spectral maw where his mouth was supposed to be.

"The abyss," he said in a rumbling voice. He sat down next to me all the while continuing to stare at Franny, a quarter his size, who returned his look without fear. The abyss spoke again. "Every man is an abyss . . . ," he said deliberately, like some bleak prophet. "Frozen into steel, a man labors all day . . . but crossing the river, he falls."

I was certain he was insane. To break the tension, I said, "Well, yeah, it's like that, isn't it?" He turned slowly, acknowledging my existence for the first time. He looked at me the way a man might look at a fly just before smashing it on the table. His forearms were bigger around than my neck. Maybe he was the fierce avenging angel of the goose I had killed, here to mete out my penance.

"Hey, he was only kidding," Louie said, deflecting his attention. "He didn't mean anything by it."

The mountain looked at Louie and then at Franny again. I wasn't afraid for her, though. If it really came down to it—if Franny got fired up—she could stare down a brown bear. What's more, she'd make a huge scene, and a posse would be at her side in no time, ready to defend her. I wasn't so confident about my chances, though, or Louie's, for that manner. Subterranean danger seeped from the pores of this menacing hunk of meat.

"A man . . . ," he began again slowly, as if blood oozed from his mouth. "A man crosses the great river . . . but the abyss waits."

None of us knew what to make of this.

"The abyss," he repeated. He stared at Louie a long time and then got up, turning his back as big as the night, and returned to the bar.

We didn't say a word, took one more slug of beer, and beat it out the door. Laughing to relieve the tension, we stumbled to the hotel and snuck Jake and Woody in through the back window. We all slept unsteadily that night and tried hard not to dream about the abyss.

The next day, we got up early to get to the ferry. To our astonishment and dismay, the truck had another flat. Impossible! Louie, for all his gifts and talents, had one terrible karma to bear. In some prior life, he must have run around loosening up wheels on chariots before the big races in old Rome or something. For three years and through numerous vehicles, I hadn't had one flat. Yet in one sixteen-hour period with Louie driving, we had two.

There was just enough time to get to the once-a-week Hollis ferry with about twenty minutes to spare. I jacked up the truck, and Louie hauled the flat down the street to find somebody to fix it—at 7:30 a.m. on a Sunday. Maybe we would not escape the abyss after all.

Louie found an auto-repair shed. He beat on the door of an adjoining apartment until a guy in overalls and a cap opened up. He assessed the tire, then scrunched up his face. "Them's split rims," he said. "I can't touch 'em." Split-rim wheels are made such that they need special equipment to change or they spring apart, impossible to put together by hand.

"Who can?" Louie asked.

"Maybe try JD around the corner," the guy said and closed his door.

JD turned out to be an expert on split-rim wheels. It took him twenty minutes, and we had a tire. We mounted it, waved goodbye to Craig, and hauled across the island as fast as *Trucka* could barrel us. Woody and Jake stood on opposite sides of the truck bed, their noses pointed forward, eyes blinking back the wind as we made the Hollis ferry with two minutes to spare.

Chapter 14

THE LAST TIME

November 1983

Across the sea, purple mountains pressed against the predawn sky. The ocean rose and fell peacefully as if the belly of a vast sleeping animal. For weeks, great sea winds from the southeast had slashed against the red cabin, but today a rare north breeze gentled the air. Franny and Louie had gone back to their home on Whidbey Island in Washington, and Woody and I were up early to climb Deer Mountain above Ketchikan before the snows of winter would cut off the path.

We drove through the dark, scaring up the elkhound for his futile run at Woody, who wagged a victor's dance from the truck bed. We made our way to town and up behind it to the trailhead at the base of the mountain. My boots crunched across frozen ground as splintered sun sifted through the trees and Woody's breath clouds led the way up the deserted switchbacks.

A few hours later, we reached snow at twenty-five hundred feet, and I strapped on my snowshoes. Icicles from the edge of rocks dripped with crystal light. Our tracks were the only ones visible across the virgin landscape. A half hour later, a hundred yards from the summit, we came up against a steep snow wall. Sadly, Woody would have to stay below. I took off the snowshoes and began to kick in boot holds and climbed, a bit precarious without crampons or an ice ax. One misstep and they wouldn't find my body till spring a thousand feet down.

Incredibly, as I looked behind, there was Woody coming along, pulling himself up through my boot holds. I worried for him, but his eyes radiated pure fearlessness. Paw by paw-pull, he climbed behind me. Two-thirds of the way up, we stopped to rest, and a floatplane buzzed by to investigate, the pilot waving at us—two insects clinging to the hill.

We made it to the top with hoots and hollers and had a dance under a bright royal-blue sky. The inlets and bays below shimmered like pools of mercury. Ravens flashed silver in the morning light and shouted in percussive tongues. To the south, the tiny spires of Saxman's totem poles caught the first rays of sun in the sleeping village. To the east, Ketchikan looked like nothing more than a dirt clod strewn along the green coast. Inland, mountain ranges stretched for dozens of miles while, to the north, our lighthouse sparked along the sea. Directly below, India-ink-colored lakes absorbed the light into their bottomless depths. Next to them was a scar in the landscape, a true feat of Alaskan civic intelligence: the town dump. Only Ketchikan, with thirteen feet of rain a year, would locate its dump above the city. Now I am no engineer, but doesn't rainwater seeping through trash run downhill?

The wine was good, and we stayed the day cavorting about the mountaintop before sliding down with yelps and shouts and Woody's eyes blazing glory.

As the days grew colder and the nights longer, the fireplace in the cabin sputtered on my green wood. The first full winter in the wilds had arrived, necessitating indoor sweaters and a coat, while Woody had all the covering he needed. Something else had moved in with us, however. It had been there at the beginning, hidden in the blush of spring and the long summer, obscured in the adventure of raising a new dog in a new land. A pervasive underlying loneliness that felt as old as time rose from its dormancy. It seemed as if all my life I had been running from this loneliness, always a half step behind. It had caught up now in the long, dark alone nights, Woody the only thing keeping it at bay.

He had, however, also begun to escalate his habit of dog walkabouts. I tried to keep him near me, but his soul was the soul of a free-roaming dog. Most of the time, he did stay close, but every now and then, he disappeared for long spells, pushing me on countless occasions out the door to search for him along the gravel roads, dirt driveways, and woods, but never with success.

So waiting became my curriculum. And when his single paw scratch at the back door heralded his return, he received a proper scolding. As the nights lengthened, so did my reprimands of him: a wallop to the backside, a talking to, a shake of his face. But Woody lived only in the moment, so in his dog mind, was he was being punished for coming home? There had to be a way, though, to stop these prolonged walkabouts. The more they happened, the angrier I'd get.

Eventually, we seemed to reach an understanding, and he stayed close, arresting my fall into isolation. But I hadn't accounted for windchill of twenty-five below. On the winter solstice, with night reaching its eighteen-hour zenith, Arctic winds poured down Clover Passage, freezing everything in their path. An uninsulated cabin with green firewood was no match for it. I slept beneath a wool hat, sweater, pants, and socks. The only thing that poked out of the sleeping bag below a pile of two blankets and comforter was my nose.

A few hours of ragged sleep rewarded us the next morning with a quarter inch of ice on the inside of the window. It took an ice scraper to clear off, and wonder of wonders, six inches of snow covered our world. Woody ran out, pouncing and bouncing as he raced around in circles taking bites of his first snowfall.

On the beach, we played *snowdog baseball*. He was Johnny Bench sitting behind home plate. Twenty yards away on the mound, the pitcher scraped his foot a few times and looked to Johnny for the signal for the next pitch. He waved off the first, agreed with the second, and nodded his head. Checking the runner at first, the pitcher went into his windup, and hurled a fastball that exploded in Johnny's dog-mitt mouth. Johnny jumped at every pitch and never missed one. The invisible ump called strikes and balls until we retired the side while blue waves whipped below the reef.

That afternoon, the snow had melted off enough to allow a hike to the end of the road. After chopping more sad-looking firewood, I got ready to go and whistled for Woody. He had disappeared.

Dammit!

Over the next three hours, I got more steamed up until the afternoon passed, and by three o'clock, it was already deep night. There'd be no sign of daylight until ten the next morning. Searching for Woody proved useless as always, and, angrily, I stomped back to the cabin.

An hour later, there it was: the single paw scratch at the back door. I stormed over, ripped it open, and pulled him in by his collar. *Damn you!* I yelled, pushing him down on his side and spanking him on his rump as the anger grew. *Don't run away. Stop running away!* I muttered through clenched teeth as each hit gained momentum. It didn't feel like it was enough, however, so I impulsively reached over and grabbed a piece of cedar kindling and raised it above him. A cold, righteous anger flooded into me.

Then I looked down into his eyes. Woody just lay there taking the hits . . . just taking the hits. He didn't struggle, or express an ounce of blame or anger at what I was doing . . . just pain. *Just taking the hits.*

In that moment, with the piece of kindling poised above him, I suddenly felt we were not alone. My dad appeared. The ragged current of his fear ran inside my own veins like an icy creek.

The only memory of his touch was being bent over his knee, facedown, without a clear idea of why, my body waiting for each wallop, paralyzed. I felt for the first time the frustration and fear that had propelled his hand: the disappointments of his life, the fear of not being in control, perhaps even the fear of losing me.

I was frustrated at not being in control and terrified of losing Woody, the creature closer to me than any, and that fear wore the face of anger. Appalled, I dropped the kindling to the hearthstones and lay down next to him and held him. *I am so sorry, amigo. I am so, so sorry. Be free, sweet one. Be free . . .* As tears welled behind my eyes, I vowed to never hit him again.

It was a pledge I fulfilled to the end of our days together.

Chapter 15

YOU BE BY US

March 1984

Trucka de la Ducka barreled toward Saxman with Woody riding shotgun, watching the road. The rain beat down along the Narrows, grim and impenetrable. A perpetual shower of three weeks had sopped everything. *Intrepid*, a slate-gray purse seiner, plowed toward Wrangell against the wind like a messenger from the underworld. A pair of ravens careened over the murky evergreens of Pennock Island.

Entering Saxman, opposite the sun-raven totem pole, Delores Strong, the village matriarch, walked along the road in the rain with her cane. As she looked up and recognized my truck, she stopped and turned her back on me until we drove by. Then she rotated around and continued up the road as before.

It had been this way for nearly a year now, the elders in the village treating me as an outcast or, worse, invisible. It was difficult to be a white guy in an Indian town and an accountant at that, but to also have people turn their backs bit me to the core.

We turned up the hill from the highway, Woody's head out the window, nosing a wet mélange of backyard dogs and mangy puppies. At the top, we passed by the largest collection of totem poles in the world, some twenty-six in all. Carved by Alaskan Natives in the early 1930s, the poles were copies of originals from the abandoned villages of Tongass and Cape Fox.

Saxman was the child of an arranged marriage of those two villages. By the 1880s, smallpox had devastated the Tongass and Cape Fox people down to a handful, and whiskey sellers had come in to do their share. Samuel Saxman, a Presbyterian minister, visited the remnants of the villages "to help lead the children to Jesus." He wanted to start a new home for them with a church and school. The villagers, a hundred from Cape Fox and seven hundred from Tongass, were amenable to the move. The Tlingit shamans, those who hadn't died already, couldn't compete. Jesus was the promise of a new life, and the white folks seemed to be doing fine by him. One village leader told me, reflecting on that time, "This character of Jesus actually made some sense—a new savior amid the collective horror of our losses."

Samuel Saxman never got to see his dream come true, however. He was paddling up the coast, looking for a village site with Native teacher Louis Paul and clan leader Wah-Koo-Se. A December storm swept in, and the men were lost, their canoe wrecked on the rocks.

Seven years later, the location of the new village was set, and it was named after the lone white man in the canoe. About 350 people now lived in Saxman, and an uneasy distrust had developed between the Cape Fox and Tongass peoples. Even though most of the poles and most of the original inhabitants had been Tongass, over time, the village had taken on more of a Cape Fox identity. The Tongass people were made to feel progressively unwanted. Most had resettled in nearby Ketchikan.

I felt a bit of what the Tongass people must have felt. Not welcomed here, at least not by the elders. The image of Delores turning her back to me burned into my heart.

Two weeks later, everyone at Cape Fox went to a potlatch. It was to be held in an old clan house, a rickety building on stilts with a large, faded halibut design on the front. A short, unstable ramp led to a big meeting room with a linoleum floor overlooking the bay. Long folding tables were covered with paper tablecloths and wildflower arrangements. The potlatch was a one-year memorial for Joe Johnson, one of Saxman's elders. Potlatches, or *parties*, as the Saxman folks called them, were held after forty days and again one year after loved ones had passed away. Photos of Joe, his Chilkat dance robe, ceremonial staff, and a cedar headdress were displayed on a table. As Joe was a member of the Eagle moiety, by tradition, the Raven side prepared, cooked, and served all the food.

Leonard, one of Delores's many grandkids, a stout teen sporting a shy smile, came over to me.

"Junior says for you to sit over here." He pointed to a seat at one of the guest tables.

There were a lot of people called Junior in the village. You figured out which one by who was talking to you. In this case, it was Leonard's dad, Junior DeWitt. If I had a primary ally in the village, it was him. Junior always met me with a laugh or a joke, and his family had embraced me from the beginning, having me over to their house many times.

I took a seat at a long table.

"You want pop or juice?" Leonard asked.

"Juice'll be fine, Leonard."

An older man up front was speaking Tlingit into a microphone. He went on and on, his speech emotionally charged,

almost theatrical, rising in pitch as if he were calling to someone in a tree deep in the forest.

Leonard returned with some orange Kool-Aid in a
Styrofoam cup.

"Get a plate, join the line," he said.

Two long tables were arrayed with platters from the
kitchen. The air was pungent with cooked fish and fried foods.
While I waited, the old man finished speaking, and a few people clapped. An elderly woman then walked to the mic and
began speaking also in Tlingit, punctuated by a host of gut-
tural clicking noises from her throat, reminding me of some of
the sounds ravens made in the woods.

In the old days, potlatches were village parties that celebrated births, rites of passage, weddings, funerals, or penance
for some shameful event—a public act of apology. The US and
Canadian governments saw potlatches as the most formida-
ble of all obstacles in "assimilating the heathens," so they were
outlawed in the 1880s based on reports from missionaries that
the parties incited debauchery and idleness and were contrary
to "civilized values."

The Saxman potlatch was oriented around gift giving, long
speeches, dances, and lots of food. There was smoked salmon,
herring eggs on kelp, dried seaweed, mashed potatoes, halibut,
blueberries, salmonberries, soapberries, and Indian fry bread.
I filled a plate and made my way back to the table. The best
surprise were the herring eggs, crunchy white dots on kelp that
tasted of salt.

"Where is that white dog of yours?" came a voice behind
me. It was Willie, Delores's youngest. Everyone called him
Junior.

"He's out in the truck."

"I never seen you two apart," he said with a stub-toothed
grin.

Another voice joined in. "Hey, who you callin' a white dog?" It was Junior DeWitt, putting his arm around me protectively. The two "Juniors" laughed long and hard, repeating it over and over, "Who you callin' a white dog!" both of them exploding in laughter each time.

Dancers were now performing a slow, mournful dance, the women swaying from one foot to the other, accompanied by a single drumbeat and chanting. They wore black-and-red button blankets with clan emblems of Bear, Eagle, Beaver, or Wolf sewed on the backs. The men wore headdresses and revolved around, as if their blankets were wings, making loud calls: *Whoooo! Whooo!* When it ended, the dancers slowly turned their backs to display their house crests.

Leonard came up to me again. "Gram wants to see you." He waited for me to stand up. *Who was Gram?*

He led me to the elder's table, where a group of ten men and women in their seventies and eighties sat with faces as wrinkled as tree bark. Delores rotated her head toward me, and then gestured to the seat next to her. She said four simple words.

"You be by us."

Sitting down, not much was said. The elders did not look at me directly, but they seemed aware of my presence. They spoke mostly in Tlingit with a smattering of English mixed in. Teenagers came by and placed white Styrofoam cups in front of us, inside of which was some grayish-colored goop. The elders delighted in it like it was ice cream. It smelled a bit rancid, but now was not the time to be squeamish, and I shoved a spoonful into my mouth.

I nearly gagged and struggled to swallow whatever this was. My dismay was visible, as one by one, the elders began to laugh, looking at me with the most mischievous faces.

"What," I gasped to Delores, "is it?"

"Seal grease," she replied.

It tasted like Vaseline that had been left out in the tide for three days. Denton, the chief, said something in Tlingit. Everyone laughed. It seemed the whole room was bubbling at my expense.

"He says you're a real Indian now," Delores translated, "cuz you're red in the face." The laughter moved through the congregation in waves as people told and retold the joke. I felt I had passed through some kind of an initiation.

Back at my table, Junior DeWitt told me that the elders would often keep their distance from newcomers to the village until they got a clearer measure of who someone was. They had been receiving reports of me over the year and watching, a kind of hidden consensus-building network.

"Maybe passed the test, huh," I said.

"Yeah, you did—for now," he replied. "Not bad for a white dog." And he laughed and laughed, a rollicking cackle that wrapped me inside like a warm blanket.

Chapter 16

DELORES

March 1984

Two weeks later, Leonard showed up at the Cape Fox office.

"Gram wants to see you," he said.

Delores's house was a tumbledown two-story next to the highway, streaked with white primer and blue overcoat. A small, pitiful-looking dog was tied up on a short rope under the porch. The yard sported a rusty tricycle, rounds of fire-wood, piles of tossed-out clamshells, and a tarp over garden tools. Smoke eased from the chimney as I walked up the steps and knocked on the door. It pushed open on its own. Delores was in the kitchen.

"Come in," she said, moving slowly and pulling out a plas-tic-covered chair from the table. The kitchen was cluttered but clean and smelled of cooked rice. In the living room, a small boy sat on the floor, eyes glued to the TV.

The living room was unadorned and tidy. It had a few old couches and recliners arranged along the walls with a couple coffee tables and lamps between. Twenty people could fit in, and did often for family meetings. A carved canoe paddle with a beaver design hung above one wall, and cedar baskets and family photos were arrayed in a glass case.

"You want coffee?" she asked.

"Sure, that would be good," I said, not really wanting it. Coffee gave me the jitters. She placed a Tongass Trading mug in front of me and set out a plate of store-bought sugar cookies.

"So, who is the dog under the porch?" I asked.

"That dog!" she exclaimed. "He barks all the time. Can't keep him quiet. Willie, he gave it to me." After a pause, she repeated, "That dog."

"Have you seen Woody? He gets away sometimes and runs around the village."

"That white dog," she scoffed. "He's never away from you. Maybe you married that dog." She laughed and put two spoonfuls of sugar in her coffee.

"Junior calls me White Dog now," I said.

She chuckled again. Angela, one of her teenage grandkids, came in with her boyfriend. Angela's daughter followed and plopped down in front of the TV.

"Larry's car broke down," Angela said to Delores. "We're goin' to pick him up at Tatsuda's."

"We're havin' a meetin' later," Delores told them as they disappeared out the door. She looked out the window. Her eyes were gray like the sea on a turbid day, her hair wispy and white. Delores had a large round face, with fleshy jowls that hung into a frown that added to her imperial bearing.

Across the Narrows, white mists rose from the hemlock trees while seagulls rolled through the air. Occasional car tires whistled along the wet pavement, mixed with the strident blare of the TV. Delores sipped at her coffee.

"I was sittin' at Joe's party," she said. "He used to get us together." Long silences punctuated her speaking. "It was him

that kept the songs alive. At gatherin's . . . used to happen a lot."
She looked again distantly out the window. The phone rang,
and somebody in the back answered it.

"There's a way things are *done*," she said. "The old ways.
Joe knew 'em. The elders back then. They passed these down to
us. A certain way *you do things*." She spoke with a musical lilt,
punctuated with a passionate emphasis.

"People today don't *know*." She looked down at her hands,
seventy years of hard work in them. "My kids go around, get in
trouble. Talk back all the time. People don't respect now."

She got up and refilled our coffees, though mine was hardly
touched.

"These songs, these are *our* songs." She gestured out the
window. "You go up Wrangell, Klawock, they got their own
songs up there. These songs come down to *us*."

Unsure of the reason for my summons, I sipped the thin
coffee and stayed mostly quiet, saying just enough to keep her
talking.

"It's sad. I feel sad about Joe," she said softly.

"When did you learn the songs?"

"From the start. Doris, Wilma, Joe, Alice Young, they all
taught us kids. Taught us the songs, the dances. When people
came over from Klawock, or down from Klukwan, Wrangell,
or Sitka, we performed at the parties."

"Do you teach them now?" One of the white sugar cookies
exploded in my mouth.

"I teach my own kids. But it's hard. They don't want to
learn. Rather watch TV. No one speaks the language no more,"
she said sadly.

In her early life, Delores's family would move to a remote
camp in the summers to gather deer and seal meat, salmon,
and berries. She grew up speaking Tlingit but, at eight, was
sent away to a boarding school in Sitka and punished for
speaking her language. It was fifty years before she spoke it

again. She got married, but her husband died of alcohol-fueled liver failure in his late thirties.

I asked her about Cape Fox, what she felt about it.

"All I see is shiny new pickups," she said. "Comin's and goin's from that office. Who *pays* for them? Whose gettin' *them*?" Her voice rose.

"It's good, though, the distributions, right?" I asked. "And some jobs?"

Delores grew agitated. "Whose *gettin'* them jobs, can you tell me? We get checks, time to time. A few blueberries from the bushes."

A stream of some of Delores's eight kids, twenty grandkids, and four great-grandchildren filtered into the house, and the kitchen filled up. It was time for me to get back to work, feeling a little sick from the coffee and sugar cookies.

The visit with Delores kept circling in my mind like a carousel. She hadn't asked me anything, just told me stories. A few days later, Woody had taken up residence in my office doorway, upside down, asleep on his back, his balls splayed out and jowls hanging open. Anyone who visited me had to step over him. As quiet as a pin drop, I whispered across the room, *Vamos.* His eyes flicked open as if he had heard the blast of a foghorn. He rolled over, ready as always to go outside.

We walked out of the Cape Fox grounds along the upper lot. Ahead was the big red box of the community hall and the totem park. Woody ran among the totems, perfumed a couple of them with raised leg, and disappeared into the nearby evergreens. I sat along the frog-design retaining wall, their rotted cedar heads poking out.

Most of the totems had a dominant figure at the top, an eagle, raven, wolf, or bear. My favorite was the Abraham Lincoln pole, with his beard and black top hat. It supposedly commemorated an event from the late 1880s. Two Tlingit villages at war were visited by the revenue cutter USS *Lincoln*, whose captain helped broker a peace between them. In honor of that event, Tongass Village carved the Lincoln pole. There he stood now, a lone white man atop a pole, looking out at the Narrows into some unknown future.

Down the road sat the Rock Oyster Boy totem, squatting on his haunches with his hand stuck in the mouth of a creature. It represented the tale of a village boy who, foraging for food in the tide, got his hand caught in the mouth of a huge oyster. His family tried to pull him out, and as the tide rose, they gave him the bladder of a seal filled with air so he could breathe underwater—but his was a cruel fate and he drowned. He sits now, his fist pinned forever inside the oyster by the side of the road.

Just then, an idea arose. Delores had talked a lot about wanting the young ones to learn the songs and dances. I headed back to Delores's house and walked up her steps. She was in the kitchen as usual.

"Delores, if we could create something, a way for you to regularly teach the grandkids the songs and dances again, do you think we could allow other people to come and see?"

The village had over 45 percent unemployment. Two miles up the road, in Ketchikan, tourists poured off big cruise ships like ants. Maybe we could bring a little economy to Saxman.

She didn't say anything.

I was on unsteady ground. This wasn't my home. This wasn't my village, my culture. I kept talking to cover my uncertainty. "If we did it so that you could teach exactly the way you want . . . without being interfered with . . . and, uh, people just get to watch respectfully." I shrugged my shoulders.

I wasn't sure if she understood, nor was I so sure myself, arranging the bones of an idea with no meat on it. She looked

out her window for some time. In the living room, the omni-
present TV blared. Then she said simply, "That might be okay."

That was the closest to a *yes* you would ever get out of
Delores.

Chapter 17

A HOLE IN THE ROOF

Late Fall 1984

The day rose crystalline and clear, and despite the immaculate calmness of the sea, an uneasy, nervous energy bundled in my midriff. After my visit to Delores, the work at Cape Fox had taken on a new anxiety, away from the accounting regimen into the business of creating a cultural tourism village in Saxman. I had no experience in doing anything like it, and was out of my depth and culture, and it was too early to expect encouragement from anyone else. I also felt anxious about the upcoming winter—and of being alone.

Woody got up from his yellow recliner and wandered over to roust me from bed with his big black muzzle looming and tail slowly wagging: *Time to go outside, man.* I grabbed his forelegs and wrestled him onto the futon, threw the covers over his dog body, and rolled out, leaving him tangled in sheets. He slid to the bottom and into the open just in time to see me going out the door with my shirt half on, heading for the beach. Woody passed me before the top of the rickety stairs and clambered down the steps, faster than an eight-year-old on his way to the den.

The sea thrummed against the black rocks and gulped into crevices. An impenetrable monthlong cloud cover had lifted, and it felt like waking up on a new planet. Islands across from the cabin, shrouded for weeks, appeared as if just then created. The breeze carried a hint of vinegar and seaweed, and cold, pristine air passed into my appreciative lungs. We hoofed a ways up a beach devoid of humans. Woody nosed through clumps of kelp, starfish, and mussel shells. I threw a stick far to sea, and he crashed into the waves, paddling out to nab it, and—impersonating a large sunken rat—emerged from the surf, shook off, and raced down the shore.

The sun tipped sharp and clear over the evergreens. Trying to kick the knot from my belly, with a little yell, I stomped the ground and took off on a beach race, but Woody roared by and beat me soundly. The victor came back to lick the loser's face, bent over at the finish line, sucking for air. We cut through the woods, my lungs aching from a good run in the cold. At the dirt road, we walked the mile back to the cabin.

In the kitchen, I made toast and Woody gulped down slugs of water. He looked up at me with long, gooey globs dripping from his jowls and his face shining. Woody's eyes radiated eternal spring, every day—eyes that brimmed with the same galactic energy that propelled planets through space, the force that turned leaves to gold in the fall and caused salmon to leap upstream. Woody lived outside of time, full on, carnal, in the moment, satisfied, connected to the elements, and devoid of shame. He was free of the scaffolding of doing and striving and desiring and worrying and ambitions I had built around myself.

He climbed up on his mustard-colored armchair, turned around in two circles, plopped down, sighed once, and was asleep in ten seconds. How I admired that! Despite living amid one of the most beautiful places in the world, obsessive thoughts and a nameless anxiety dogged my body. How lovely it would be to just scratch at my sheets a couple times, circle, and flop down fast asleep.

On this rare clear day, maybe it was time to stop putting off fixing the hole in the roof. The Little Red Cabin's decrepit stone fireplace sent most of the heat right up the stack. A woman in Saxman had given me an old woodstove, inspiring me to tear down the chimney to install it. But the work had been interrupted, and in the chimney's place, a ragged hole in the roof gaped to the sky, temporally covered with Visqueen.

I tossed wood and tools onto the low roof and hopped up, tore away the Visqueen patch, and set to frame a box for the pipe to fit through. Carpentry was not in my skill set, but when pressed to it, I could manage crudely. After twenty minutes of sawing and pounding, I noticed Woody down below in the woods sitting on his haunches, watching my every move.

A raven let go a croaky rasp from a spruce, which reverberated through the woods in the sun-sparked air. A towering spruce snag, *the devil tree*, loomed a hundred feet over the cabin like a dark totem, eerie and beautiful. The upper limbs of the surrounding evergreen trees jostled slightly in the wind. I jumped down and hefted Woody up for his first tour of the roof. Back up top, I inserted the asbestos pipe into the sleeve and balanced it while putting the flashing around, and searched for the screwdriver to tighten the collar. There it was thirty feet away. If I took my hands off the tall metal pipe, it would tumble down into the woods.

Hugging the pipe to my chest, I said, *Woody. Bring it!*, while pointing at the screwdriver with my free hand. He looked at my pointing finger and wagged his tail. I jabbed my arm back and forth and pointed behind him, *Bring it!* He looked around and took a few steps that way, then turned his triangle head back to me, tail brushing the air, slow and serious. *Bring it here!* I said more emphatically. He took a few more steps that way and pounced on a piece of two-by-four. *No! No!* I pointed strenuously beyond him. He went over to another piece of wood, half-heartedly tried it out, and looked up at me. *No!* I yelled. There were about a dozen objects spread over the roof. He investigated one after the other, and with me screaming at him to get the screwdriver, he hopped right over it and put his mouth around the handle of a hammer. *No!*

It was time to try something desperate. While picturing the screwdriver in my mind and driving out all other thoughts, I told Woody mentally to bring it to me. Maybe it was a true case of cross-species psychic communication, or simply because he had tried everything else on the roof, but he picked that screwdriver right up and brought it over. I hooted and howled and, in my excitement, reaching out to hug him, let go of the stovepipe, which rolled off the roof and dropped into the woods with a clang. I laughed, and Woody seemed to also with his eyes. *Go get the stovepipe, buddy.*

Standing up to stretch, my lower back was hurting and I didn't feel well. Suddenly weary, I walked over to the ocean side of the roof and lay down. Woody came over and sat beside me. The sun shattered on the sea and made a sparking yellow brick road directly to us. A gillnetter chugged past the lighthouse. The heat from the black roof shingles sank into my sore back and sacrum.

The sky was cloudless, a luminous, liquid blue. Eyes closed, I tried to blow away the tension that still clung to my body and felt exhausted—at being with myself, of the struggles of Saxman, of fears about the oncoming winter.

That night, the rains came and, with them, a horrible sore throat. Water began pooling on the floor from the roof hole, and my condition worsened and progressed into the dark flu they called the Ketchikan crud. Like a plague, it bloomed virulently a few times a year across the island. In a week, a third of the schools would empty; at work, someone would come down with it, give it to someone else, who would bring it back around again to you just as you were getting over the first bout. It was like living inside a giant petri dish.

There was nothing to do but lie dismally all day on my futon and watch the gray light fade into night. The darkness felt palpable, as if soaked in crude oil. The rain continued without a break. My body wrapped inside a sleeping bag and feverishly covered in blankets against the thirty-eight degrees inside the cabin, my head felt like it weighed forty pounds. Every now and then, I made a trip to the outhouse in the rain. Getting food for Woody took all my strength.

Alone in the dark, free and broken. I had progressively weaned myself from Boxtown and now lived without watch, telephone, running water, or plumbing. For months, I discouraged visitors to the red cabin, reveling in the freedom of being alone, without obligations, without a need to prove myself or explain myself or be liked.

Now, with no ability to contact anyone and no immediate neighbors, if I died, they wouldn't discover the body for a week. As my sickness stretched into its second day, towels on the floor soaked up the rain pouring through the roof. The porch door stayed open for Woody to come and go as he pleased. Most of the time, he stuck around checking in on me, looking down, soft-eyed and gentle. We took many naps together.

It was hard to remember what it was like being well. The sickness seemed eternal. It felt like those little demons you see from medieval drawings chewing on a body. My head ached too much to read, and because I slept a lot during the day, a good portion of the night, the only entertainment was the lighthouse sweeping through the cabin like an atomic blaze. I counted the seconds between the flashes. *One thousand one,*

one thousand two, one thousand three, one thous— Every three and a half seconds, the lighthouse clicked through a frame from an infinite, slow-motion film playing on the walls of the pitch-black cabin.

The wind whipped the trees, and the rain spoke in endless monotones. In my feverish mind, I began to imagine a terrifying beast coming down the woods along the path, toward the cabin. Every flash of the lighthouse, he crept nearer. His face was horrible, a bit like the devil's in *The Exorcist*, a movie that terrified me as a teenager. Demonic possession still frightened me. A force was coming down the trail, unstoppable, horribly evil, that would not only destroy me but also inhabit my soul.

At each flash of light, he drew nearer. Despite my mind trying desperately not to think of him, he stared at the cabin from the woods. There was a lighthouse flash, and a creak on the porch floor. The door opened. A flash, and there he was in the kitchen looking in at me. Darkness. *Three and half seconds.* Another burst of light, and he was partway across the room, the deviant face, unspeakably evil, closer each time the room lit up. A leering face, coming toward me . . . I yelled in delirium, *Woody, Woody!*

With the rain still pouring through the hole in the roof, Woody's face stood over me in the dark. He nosed me aside and crawled into bed and pressed his body against mine. He would bark if the devil came. He would protect me. My face pressed into his fur, miraculously, fitfully, I slept.

Chapter 18

DRUMBEATS AT THE FRONTIER

Summer 1985

An eight-story floating hotel pulled up to Ketchikan's dock. Running the length of ten football fields and carrying three thousand passengers, the *Royal Princess* cruise ship began to disgorge its cargo into a town only a dozen blocks around. As the mostly retirement-age people slowly descended the ramp to the dock, the Cape Fox Dancers met them in their regalia, singing a traditional welcome song. Delores and three of her daughters, two of her sons, four grandchildren, and one great-grandchild swayed back and forth in their clan crests of Beaver, Raven, and Halibut, while the drumbeat welcomed the people to shore. Delores was in front instructing the little ones, only four years old, in the proper steps.

In the old days, when a canoe filled with people of peaceful intent arrived from another village, it would first ask permission to land. The villagers would shout back to them and sing a song of welcome. This modern welcoming ceremony was my first naive idea to get tourists to eventually come the two and a half miles to Saxman from Ketchikan. If successful, it could launch a self-sustaining cultural village, owned by the Saxman people. Except for the stray taxis that brought people to the totem park, tourists rarely came to Saxman.

It took me a while to talk Delores and the dancers into venturing into Ketchikan. Until this morning, I wasn't sure if any of them would show up. But here they were with drum and song to welcome the visitors, who walked by smiling at the children until corralled into buses and hauled away on sightseeing adventures.

I didn't really know what I was doing. The dancers, though, trusted me, and this was a start. Delores wanted a way to encourage the younger ones to get more involved in the culture, and the dance group needed money to make bead blankets and dance regalia and to travel to other communities to perform and to host gatherings in Saxman.

The Frontier Saloon was a bawdy local drinking hole in the middle of town. Nighttimes, it featured an eclectic entertainment lineup such as a local melodrama, *The Fish Pirate's Daughter*; women's mud wrestling; or a rock 'n' roll show. During the day, it was mostly empty and often closed.

I talked the owners into opening midday and having the dance group perform for tourists on cruise-ship days. The kids walked around town in their dance regalia, handing out flyers. Woody took up residence by the front door where the bartender set out a water dish and supplied him a healthy ration of pepperoni sticks.

The dancers performed to groups of eight to thirty people. Sawdust kicked up from the floor mixed with the slightly sour smell of last night's beer. Despite the tavern surroundings, which caused the dancers and me some embarrassment, they gave it everything they had, transforming the space with power and commitment to the dance.

Back at Cape Fox, accounting was not yet in my rearview mirror. As contrary as it was to my nature, if channeled right, debits and credits could shed light on chaos and poor planning. I decided to do an analysis of the timberlands and company assets to compare it to the enormous debt that Sisewell had taken on. My report made it clear: in order to retire the debt and pay for Sisewell's projects, plus staff, management, and overhead, the company was going to have to log off nearly all its timberlands. Sisewell was taking Cape Fox off a cliff, and no one realized it.

The president of the company, Ben David, and lands manager Sam Winston and I met and decided to do something not often done in business—to take on our boss. Backed by my numbers, we put our jobs on the line and went over Dave's head to the board. This caused a great deal of upheaval. The board felt betrayed; they had done what they had to do: faced with overseeing an unfamiliar organization and corporate structure, they had dutifully hired who they believed was a trusted and capable guy to manage the millions of dollars in land and money entrusted to the corporation. Sisewell had the best of intentions, but he had little if any viable experience or track record doing any of these kinds of projects or managing a start-up logging company. He was rolling huge dice with other people's money, and his plans weren't working. The Tlingits were left holding the bill.

Our efforts led eventually to Dave's resignation. He had, however, written himself a lucrative employment contract with a large payout and ten acres of Native-owned land. He got his reward, the equipment manufacturers got theirs, as did the banks, lawyers, and loggers. The shareholders got a handful of jobs, a few large distribution checks, and a corporation mired in debt.

We had to work overtime to sell off equipment, close down the sawmill and other unproductive assets, and fire most of the employees. Logging would have to continue for a number of years just to pay the enormous loans to finance unprofitable subsidiaries and a hotel project no more than a parking lot on a hill. After it was done, nearly twelve thousand acres of pristine forest lay clear-cut. By 1990, the rest of the twenty thousand acres would be gone.

Sisewell's gambles did not bode well for the relationship between the dancers and me. Here they were being asked to trust another white guy, one asking them to dance in a Ketchikan saloon, no less. It took many late nights at Delores's to keep an uneasy peace.

Chapter 19

WHAM-O DOG

August 1986

I was jarred awake in the aimless dark . . . What was that? There
it was again, a sound that my waking brain struggled to name
. . . then it became clear: *The fucking rooster.* Another grating,
throat-clearing gargle ripped through the air. Its origin was
my neighbors, Steve and Dawn. In the search for solitude, I
was learning, the biggest obstacle was neighbors. Hidden by a
thicket of trees and a long way from the Little Red Cabin, their
house was perched on the face of a rock cliff. But over the past
year, they had progressively knocked and drilled and cleared
enough space on the cliff to house a few farm animals—small
horses, pygmy goats, and most recently, chickens. The rooster
was a nightmare, along with Steve's early-Sunday-morning
chain-saw work.

On the porch with a coffee, the sun not yet up, I began to
think of the many ways to assassinate the rooster. The sea air
was breezing softly. Woody was sleeping in, hanging upside

down from his mustard-yellow recliner, his head off the end, snoring. I got him up for an early-morning adventure.

As waves whispered against the shore, Woody and I stepped across the barnacled rocks and sand of the beach. The dark-dawn mirror of a tide pool held the pregnant moon. *God is beauty*, I thought. Maybe nature is creation's need to express the divine beauty of its soul. The pool's serenity invited me to sit and listen to the soft undertones of the ocean's sway against the earth. Woody sat by, calm and content, as if this were the most natural thing in the world to do—to be in no hurry, to just lounge, breathe, and gaze at the world, entranced.

A whistle from a bald eagle pierced the dawn. Sitting there, I considered the mystery of this dog. What was it that connected us? He'd sit with me here for three days if I stayed or follow me down the beach in a second if I got up, constellating around me without having to say a word.

In the eastern sky blazed Sirius, the Dog Star, the brightest celestial body and part of the constellation Canis Major, "the Greater Dog." Some mystery schools consider Sirius to be *the sun behind the sun* and, therefore, the true source of our sun's potency. Sirius is also thought to be the celestial birth canal, the star-gate through which all souls pass to be here and, afterward, through which we return to source. Woody did feel like a celestial visitor to me, jettisoning through a cosmic window, destined to be my companion.

I dug my hand deep into his coat, and he lifted his snout to the sky and, with half-closed eyes, exhaled deeply. *Body to body. Touch.* I was raised in a family where touch was not sanctioned, the body an object to be avoided. I was taken by nurses at the moment of birth and don't recall my mother ever touching me skin to skin. From teenage years on, touch, if any, was only a precursor to sex, and that sex was divorced from feeling or awareness. Nurturing touch, what was that? Touching

Woody, I felt a warm mammalian closeness, being to being, medicine for a traumatized soul.

The slightest breeze brushed my face with the scent of kelp and cedar. Above my head, the trees rustled as the eagle lifted and slow-winged its way into the opening day. Gold-white streaks of sun sifted through the treetops; the ocean shimmered and the air crackled with salt. A seal popped its gray head up and periscoped around before settling its dark eyes on us. Woody looked back as if he were seeing a long-lost cousin.

The rising sun cried out for an early ritual of Frisbee. Woody was now a champion Wham-O dog. As light broke over the trees, he raced down the sand and snatched a short toss easily out of the sky, then jogged it back, the Frisbee offered from his snout. I loved elongating this moment. Slowly, my hand inched down toward him. This caused his tail to stop wagging and a serious concentration to overcome him. Ever so tenderly and gravely, he let me take the Frisbee from his mouth, his eyes ever riveted upon it. The disc was all there was in the world, *the still point at the center of the dance.*

The tide pool shimmered. A heron squawked. Woody's breath formed vapor clouds in the morning air. He waited as a runner for the gun, as a lover heightened before the rush to ecstasy, a Saturn V rocket in its tower, liquid oxygen steaming from its vents.

Ya, I whispered emphatically, and Woody blasted off across the beach. At the same time, my arm drew back and my right leg stepped forward. The Frisbee made a slight *whish* sound as it left my hand and flew five feet off the ground, over Woody's head, sailing long down the beach.

Woody's paws pounded on the earth, drubbing as one rhythmic unit—*thumpa-thumpa-thumpa-thump*. The Frisbee, thirty yards ahead, arcing toward the ocean, seemed out of his reach. But like chasing a rabbit, he instantly calculated the trajectory and angled himself slightly toward its destination as he

ran. The disc was six feet away and descending now only a foot
off the water's surface. Then in one burst of Greater Dog, he cut
quick to the water, extended his neck, and leapt full-chested
into salt spray.

CxcchK... Echoing through the morning came the sound
of hard spinning plastic arrested by canine teeth. Everything
disappeared underwater but his head and the Frisbee. To
whoops and hollers from the beach, he swam back in and loped
up to me with a James Bond confidence in his eye. His teeth
chattering on the disc's edge, he invited me to reach down for
it again, which I did as slowly as possible. Seawater drained off
his sleek body, every cell and muscle radiant and alert. His car-
rot-brown eyes were ablaze and locked on to mine. And inside
each of those dog-eyed globes was a tiny image of me.

Chapter 20

LAST NIGHT AT THE LITTLE RED CABIN

Fall 1986

It was our last day in the Little Red Cabin. The owner was tearing it down to build a modern place. Heartache began to seep through my veins. The Little Red Cabin felt part of me; it had been the laboratory for slowly shedding the shackles of society and stepping into a more elemental existence.

On our last afternoon, we wandered through a landscape that had become ingrained. Each tree, the stones on the beach, the lighthouse, the black reef were landmarks in the *songlines* of this place. When you are alone for long enough, the objects around you take on an animism and can fill you with transcendent meaning. The Little Red Cabin was a companion, a co-conspirator in a great living secret only known by me. Each detail of its landscape had formed part of my interiority.

Grief was mingled with joy and awe at all this beauty and character we soon would have to depart. To realize the cabin's fate was to be torn down, as were doomed the dozen sweet trees before the porch. To know the cabin would be replaced by another characterless modern house saddened me further. The world needs more Little Red Cabins, raw, humble guests in the landscape.

As the skies slowly darkened and the lighthouse painted time across the ocean, the last caretakers of the cabin retreated inside to the cedar aroma-warmth of the woodstove. To celebrate our last night, I gave Woody the special dinner he always got on his birthdays. It was simple and culminated in one of the most extraordinary displays of canine gastrointestinal absorption I have ever seen.

Using a can opener, I cut the top and bottom out of a can of dog chow—Woody always got better stuff for dinner; canned dog food is like junk food for dogs, but like junk food, they will gobble it up faster than a kid at Halloween. So I pressed the contents into a perfect cylinder of globby meat standing on end on a small plate and ceremoniously, ever so slowly, put the plate before Woody and stepped back.

Before it fully settled on the floor, this sucking sound akin to a vacuum cleaner emerged from deep inside Woody's core, and in one fluid movement while the sucking force continued, he bowed his snout over the meat cylinder, tilted his head back, and with three more quick sucking sounds, disappeared the entire loaf into his belly. He never chewed. It was like watching a python swallow a small mammal whole.

The whole absorption process had taken five seconds, and the full tube of meat now lay in Woody's belly ready for digestion. He looked up at me as one who has just been shown a glimpse of heaven.

In the middle of the night, I was struck by a crazy idea and pulled on rubber boots, a heavy shirt, pants, and a Mexican poncho. *Vamos, amigo!* I said to Woody. By flashlight, we clambered down the beat-up stairs to the beach and dragged my Coleman plastic canoe across the rocks. The tide was two feet below the reef, lapping quietly against it. The canoe looked a bit precarious, sliding down into the water, but Woody leapt right in and unsteadily made his way to the front. We shoved off into the night, toward the destination that had been the beacon through our red cabin years—the lighthouse, a mile away.

Woody hung his head over the gunwale, and moonlight brushed our faces as we headed into the inky unknown. The night was radiant and clear. My paddle stirred up phosphorescent sparks in the black water, while behind us, the quickly receding red cabin with its yellow lamplight seemed a candle on the shore. I knelt and J-stroked against the current directly toward the lighthouse as it flashed every three and a half seconds. Water drops from the paddle thumbed the surface. Woody stared forward like a Norse figurehead, eyes peeled, ears alert.

Things on the open water can happen fast. When we launched, it was bright and clear with only a few migratory clouds before the moon. Now a half mile from shore, a wall of fog appeared. The air grew suddenly cold, and mist enveloped us. As quick as the coming of a mountaintop storm, we were consumed in a whiteout.

Visibility shrank to twenty-five feet. It was like being under an upside-down teacup of fog. The world vanished but for the circle of water around us. The lighthouse's diffused flashes through the fog provided an eerie illumination. I lost track of where the shore was and decided to try and keep heading toward the flame, farther out to sea. The silence was palpable, broken only by the dips of my paddle in the still water. Woody raised his snout straight up, reading the night.

A distant, far-off sound pierced the dark—*Psshuaah!* I stopped paddling.

Thirty seconds later, it came again, this time a bit louder
... *Pssshhhwaah!* A gasp from a large blowhole, approaching through the fog, maybe a hundred yards away? I began to
count. *One ... two ... three ... four ... five,* up to twenty-five
before hearing it again. *Pssshhhwaah!* A whale, its large submarine heart pounding toward us. My own heart bounced in
its hold, and Woody widened his eyes and peered into the fog.

Pssshhhwaah! Closer. Small waves slapped the hollowness
of the canoe. I didn't know if I should paddle away or maybe
that would just draw attention to our presence. I assessed the
situation: It was past midnight; we were a half mile from a
shore no longer visible. No light, no life preservers, no flare,
nothing. Just my style—to launch off with little preparation or
sense that anything could go wrong. The whale was coming
straight for two little mammals in a plastic canoe locked in a
fogbank. Woody stood up, his ears jetted forward.

Pssshhhwaah ... By the diffused flashes of the lighthouse,
my eyes searched the dim water for a dorsal fin, a tail. Nothing.
I started to count. *One ... two ... three ... four ...* and got to
twelve. *Pssshhhwaah!* Enlarged by the fog, it sounded like the
labored breath of a giant wrestler running uphill.

No one knew we were out here. How long could I survive in
forty-six-degree water? Seven minutes? Woody, though, would
likely survive, or would he swim around endlessly searching
for me before succumbing and joining me in the under deep?
Pssshhhwaah! The cetacean's gasp echoed through the night,
maybe twenty-five yards away, just off the edge of the fogbank.
Then I saw it. A long, straight ebony fluke arched out of the
water, shimmering, six feet high above a sleek, streamlined
body. An adult male orca. He blew a plume of mist into the
night air before descending again, heading directly toward us.

Woody stared ahead. *Does a dog know how to pray?*

Expecting it to next rise in front of our bow, I gripped the
paddle tighter and braced my knees against the sides. Orcas

aren't known to attack humans, but the vulnerability of our situation challenged such reason. What if it made a mistake, unaware of us, and surfaced just below the canoe? Woody looked toward the whale as if to say, *Who are you?*

One . . . two . . . I reached forward and put my hand on his back. *Five . . .* Maybe it would come up directly below us. *Six . . .* Pluck Woody off the front like an hors d'oeuvre? *Seven . . .* Maybe the paddle could be a weapon . . . *Twenty-five . . . Twenty-six . . . Twenty-seven . . .* Starboard and port, I imagined the long, sleek body overturning us.

Minutes passed that felt forever. The lighthouse flashed. We rocked side to side in the canoe. Time stretched, waiting without a breath. And then as if the end of a psychological thriller, the fog slowly lifted. We didn't hear the whale again—the ocean, but a soft carpet. I raised the paddle tentatively and started back toward the Little Red Cabin. Woody glanced at me as if the world were a fantastical mystery.

The next morning, I woke to the sound of the surf over the reef and felt a slight breeze through the open porch door. Woody was asleep on his back in his mustard-colored throne, his jowls hanging to the floor. I remembered the whale as if in a dream and was suddenly filled with gratitude for being alive. Then something caught my eye. Next to the bed, two scaly yellow legs, stiff as sticks, pointed heavenward. I peeked over the edge and saw that the legs were attached to a large, very dead rooster.

Sometime during the early dawn, Woody the Dog arose and, touched, I assumed, by a providential urge to help his best friend sleep, padded stealthily through the woods and silenced the voice of the now-deceased cock, delivering it dutifully to his master's bedside as a gift.

I laughed long, sat up, and put my bare feet on the floor. Woody's eyes slowly opened. He unwound his head, got up, stretched languorously, and easy-footed over to me and dug his nose into the soft feathers of the rooster. His tail wagged slowly.

I wondered how to break the news to my neighbors, before an idea hit me . . . Maybe I wouldn't say a word. It wasn't easy, nor did I have a clue how to do it, but on our last morning in the red cabin, with the ocean as my witness, I plucked a rooster, cleaned and cooked it on a Coleman stove, and fed it to Woody bite by bite, who never seemed happier.

Chapter 21

HOOVERVILLE

Late Fall 1986

With little notice to move out of the red cabin, the only thing I could find was a slightly decrepit mobile home south of town. It was tucked behind brush and trees, at the base of a mountain about a mile from the end of the road. The place looked like a beat-up cigarette carton with tilted floors and a pervasive mildew smell. Outside was a small garden area, overgrown and neglected for years. I called the place Hooverville.

Where the Little Red Cabin had an expansive and wide view of the world, Hooverville was myopic, with small windows looking out to tangled trees and overgrown bushes. Hopefully, it would serve as a place for just a couple months until we could get back to a more remote outpost.

Our first day there, Woody wandered up a driveway toward the mountain behind Hooverville to a small house. A red-haired woman in Carhartts with a sturdy backwoods body

stood on a ladder, cleaning debris from the gutters. She looked
to be in her early thirties.

"Well, howdy do," she said, with a slight drawl a bit like a
rancher in the Old West. She climbed down from her ladder
and met me with a big smile of crooked teeth. Outgoing, but
a bit shy at the same time, she said her name was Crow. She
seemed unsure of herself, despite a certain washtub bluster.

"Howdy," I said. "This is Woody."

Crow bent down and rubbed his ears. He immediately
went into her house and headed straight to the kitchen for any
cat food. This elicited a scream, and out the door tumbled two
girls five and seven years old. The oldest, Carrie, was thin, sen-
sitive, and polite, with long, straight auburn hair. Behind her
rambled Rachel, a little fireball with intense coal-black eyes
that fixed on me right away. Her round face was dirty beneath
dark curls. She wore a pair of rubber boots with rough brown
pants tucked into them. Unsmiling, she seemed to be sizing
me up a bit.

"That dog is eating the cat food," Carrie complained, going
over to her mom.

"Sorry about that," I said. "He's a bit of his own man."

"Aw, Shady's too fat anyway," Crow said. "Do her some
good to be a little hungry. Maybe she'll get after the mice in
the walls instead of lazing around all day long."

Woody came outside then and nosed around everyone's
legs. Rachel appraised him and began to follow him around.
She picked up a tennis ball, and Woody was all hers. She threw
it down the hill, and he was after it, rounding it up, coming back
like a boomerang, and spitting it out at her feet for another go.

"Well, come on in, then," Crow said to me. "I'll feed ya
some tea and brownies."

The house was warm, the windows a bit steamed from
some soup cooking on the stove. The front windows looked
down the woods to the backside of Hooverville. Crow's living

room floor was covered in paper, crayons, children's books, and a few stray stuffed animals and dolls. A fiddle leaned against a chair. The bookshelf was full of art books. Some incredible original watercolors hung on the walls.

"Whose are those?" I asked.

"I kind of did them," Crow said, with a self-deprecation that asked for protest. "They were just something I was trying. They didn't really work out."

"You're kidding me. They are amazing."

"You think so? Nah," she said, and smiled as she made tea.

A Doc Watson song on the radio segued into a tune by the New Riders of the Purple Sage. Carrie worked on a drawing a bit self-consciously, very careful to color inside the lines. Other drawings nearby were roughly scrawled with crayon marks thrashed over the page. I figured those were Rachel's.

"Wow, you did that?" I said to Carrie. "You are really something. How did you learn to draw horses so well?" She pretended not to beam under my praise.

"I am taking drawing in school," she said.

"Well, pretty soon, you ought to be teaching the class."

Crow brought me some aromatic tea in a pot and a plate of brownies still warm from the oven.

"So, you're the new kid on the block," she said.

"Yep, sure am. Real estate values just plummeted, huh?"

"Well, nothing but white trash to begin with around here anyway," she said and looked out the window. Rachel and Woody were in their own world. A folksy-voiced woman on the radio said, "KRBD, Rainbird Community Radio."

"Rachel!" Crow yelled. "You get back in here and clean up your room. I can't even see the floor." Rachel ignored her and kept on playing with Woody. "Rachel!" Crow yelled again.

"Okay," Rachel said, and kept right on playing with Woody.

"She's as stubborn as her dad," Crow said, with a crooked grin.

"Where's he?" I asked.

"Carrie, would you go get Rachel in here," Crow said.

Carrie got up obediently. "Okay," she replied and went outside.

Crow watched her for a moment and then said, "We're just hanging on." She left the comment suspended in the air. She poured tea in my cup and then hers. "No, we had to get away," she added. "Only thing he left me was a few bruises and a last name, which I ditched."

A surprising sense of protectiveness rose in me toward Crow and her little band of woodsy girls. I drank tea and ate too many brownies until Crow had to go into town for some supplies. They all bounded into her orange Oldsmobile station wagon and choked down the driveway until it fired, Rachel and Carrie waving from the back as they disappeared down the road.

Woody and I took a walk toward a marshy lagoon beyond our dead-end road. Halfway there, a malevolent growl roiled the air. In front of a one-story house, uphill from us, a large husky, maybe 130 pounds, was shackled by a sturdy chain to a piece of rebar deep in the ground. In the driveway was a roughed-up, muddied black Dodge pickup with oversize tires. The drapes of the house were closed.

The husky's eyes intensified, and he took a run at us. The hair on Woody's back went up, and he got lower to the ground, angling a few steps toward the charging dog. The husky ran full bore with teeth snarling and lunged. When he hit the end of the chain, it lifted him off his feet and smacked him down on his side on the bare ground. It didn't faze him a bit. He got up, spitting blood and mayhem. There was murder in those black eyes. Woody stood his ground and then slowly sauntered off, nonchalantly flaunting his freedom, which maddened the husky more, lunging at his chain repeatedly.

Woody had just met his great nemesis.

We walked to the end of the road and followed a creek bed up into the woods until it petered out in some thick brush. On the way back, Woody looked for the mad dog and pranced as we walked by, inciting the husky to thrash against his chain again. *God help us if he ever breaks free,* I thought.

Chapter 22

LILLIAN OF PARNASSUS

Late Fall 1986

After settling into Hooverville, we headed to our favorite place in town, Parnassus Bookstore, on Creek Street, the elevated walkway across Ketchikan Creek where, in the old days, whores jangled gold from fishermen's jeans and city fathers' purses. We tromped up the stairs to the second-story frame house built in 1905. In its day, it was Dolly's, a cathouse. Now its madam, Lillian Ferrence, purveyed good books, not tricks. Woody trundled ahead through the door.

"Well, here you are," exclaimed Lillian's gentle voice of welcome. By the time I made it inside, Woody was wagging his tail, looking up a steep flight of stairs that led to an attic room. Each step had books stacked along both sides. Upstairs, Lillian was ferreting around. Soon, a pair of gray orthopedic shoes descended. She beamed a smile that sweetened the world. She held a bag of treats, kept especially for Woody. He always got top priority in her store.

Lillian's wispy white hair framed a round face, with large eyeglasses that magnified blue-gray eyes. She was the grandmother a lot of us never had. Yet you couldn't let her charming aura fool you. Lillian saw straight through artifice and arrogance in others and could disarm anyone with a few well-placed words and a chuckle. Though surrounded by right-wing conservatives that ran the town, Lillian remained an outlier: one of the sharpest, most outspoken, articulate political radicals ever to grace the rocky shores of Ketchikan. She often broke into laughter describing the self-serving business and civic leaders as "the dullards at the top."

Lillian handed Woody a treat that he munched loudly and then readied himself for the next one. "You should know better than to chew with your mouth open," she scolded him.

He looked at her, glad-eyed, knowing he was not to be denied. After doling out four more treats, Lillian returned the bag upstairs.

The bookstore was L-shaped, consisting of a long walk-in hallway and a main narrow room above the mouth of Ketchikan Creek that flowed beneath the Stedman Street Bridge. Lillian stepped her five-foot-two frame up onto a small, raised platform behind a counter where her cash register sat.

"It's strange, isn't it?" she said, looking at me quizzically. "I'm shrinking as I get older."

Looming above and around her, book-stuffed shelves wrapped around her like a shawl. At age sixty-five, after forty years at a state social services agency, Lillian did what she had always dreamed of—opened a bookstore.

"I don't make much money," she said. "A lot of times, I don't make any. Luckily, I have savings to get me through." She smiled. "And I have had the best time the last three years!" Her magnified eyes beamed as she added, "It is what I enjoy."

Woody took up residence on Lillian's back porch, lazily looking out over Front Street and the Narrows to the west in the yellow-cedar afternoon light. I ordered an espresso. Lillian had one of the town's first such machines. She knew coffee was not so good for me and asked rhetorically, "Do you really think you should?" She made one extra weak for me.

On the counter, the current *Ketchikan Daily News* featured one of staff photographer Hall Anderson's shots. Today's was of three boys jumping from the Stedman Street Bridge into Ketchikan Creek. Taken from behind them and above, it seemed their legs and torsos had been choreographed in an intricate ballet of falling. Body parts stuck into and out of the frame. It was pleasing to let the eye explore it. Every day, Hall treated us with a Cartier-Bresson-like image, a piece of fine art on the front page of an otherwise conservative news rag. Nearby, a rack displayed Evon Zerbetz cards, animated with her playful, powerful visions of dragonflies, ravens, and bears. A childlike joy radiated from each.

A customer approached with a book to buy. Thus began a ritual. When you brought her a book, Lillian would take it from you tenderly, look it over, and offer a thoughtful comment on it. She would then mention other works written by the same author. It was as if each book was a child of hers that you were adopting. Meanwhile, she would pause as she calculated the taxes by hand, on a small calculator, before deliberately writing out a careful receipt. Finally she would gently slide the book into a paper bag and hand it to you with the biggest smile. It charmed everyone who was lucky enough to buy a book from her. Often people would stick around talking to her for a long time.

Some King Sunny Ade played on the store stereo. Lillian was one of the few people in Ketchikan who even knew who he was—one of the premier African guitarists and singers on the planet.

"I've always had a deep appreciation for the music of other cultures," she said. "What got me started was the movie *Black*

Orpheus. When I saw that, I couldn't stay away from the music." Lillian lived in San Diego during World War II. When the sailors came to town, she'd go down to the USO and dance all night.

"One night, a man showed me the Lindy Hop and I loved it! It was ballroom dancing mostly, though, and I loved to waltz. People don't know those dances these days."

I told her about my plan to create a cultural tourism village in Saxman.

"You know," Lillian said, "a lot of people in this town want you to fail."

I was shocked. "Why?"

"Well"—she laughed—"if you succeed, if the Native people build something successful, it will fly in the face of their narrative. The city council stiff necks will get stood on their heads." She stepped off her platform and returned some books to a shelf. "I think it's about time for them to get stood on their heads, don't you?" She chuckled.

Though Saxman was only two and a half miles up the road, you didn't have to look too deep to find an undercurrent of racism in Ketchikan. It seemed nice enough masquerading as a tourist destination, fast becoming a large curio store outlet, but it masked a harsher attitude toward things liberal, non-white, or caring of the environment. Ketchikan was a pro-gun, pro-resource extraction, right-leaning, white town. Just go listen to the old-man coffee drinkers any morning at the Pioneer Café:

". . . while the Natives get to hunt or fish anywhere they want!"

"All that land and money just given to 'em."

"I don't believe in welfare. This is a democracy. People should work hard, pull their own weight."

"Hell, I'm third-generation Alaskan. We developed this place. That's just the way it goes. I don't discriminate."

I bought a card by aquatic-surrealist Ray Troll. It took Lillian five minutes to ring it up and find just the right small paper bag to carefully slip it into.

Fresh from the good coffee buzz, we descended from Parnassus and wheeled along the elevated walkway of Creek Street, with its whooshing namesake flowing beneath. The air was ripe with rotted fish. It was fall, and the humpies had run their course, fighting their way up the creek to lay eggs and roll over, gills laboring, slowly to die. Recent torrential rains had raised the creek above its normal course and, after receding, left salmon carcasses hanging in hemlock branches ten feet up. They decorated the trees along the creek like strange and macabre Christmas ornaments.

We crossed the bridge toward the library. Along a second-story porch railing of an old wood building hung a sign, *KRBD Rainbird Community Radio.* That was the radio that had been on at Crow's.

Inside, Jerry Lee Lewis was rocking. The DJ was a stout, full-bodied guy in a high school letterman jacket, shaded glasses, and a baseball cap. He called himself the Teen Angel, and he was covered in tattoos. The Teen was also the town mortician.

"What is this place?" I asked.

"It's whatever you want it to be," he said. Teen had a cryptic, wry wit about him and a voice higher than you expected, with a demented twist to it.

"Pardon me," he said. The on-air light went red, and he turned to the mic. "That's the Killer, with 'Whole Lotta Shakin' Goin' On.' You're *Cruisin' Creek Street* with me, the Teen Angel, here every Sunday noon to two. Coming up, for you churchgoers, the weekly record from hell. But first, here's 'Money Honey,' with the great Clyde McPhatter and the Drifters."

He hit the Play button on turntable two and pushed the slider up on the soundboard. The Drifters sprang to life. It was a beautiful confluence of movement and sound.

"How long you worked here?" I asked.

"It ain't work. I'm a volunteer," he said. "There's about thirty of us."

I was dumbfounded and immediately wanted to do what he was doing. "How do you become a volunteer?"

"Well, if you can keep a cool stool," he said, "you just have to take a training course. It's about twelve hours."

"You mean . . . ," I stammered. "Are you telling me that I could take a twelve-hour course and then have my own radio show?"

"That's what they tell me," he said. The Drifters were half through, and Teen was cuing up a song from his collection of the worst songs ever made for his *Records from Hell* segment. My audience with him had come to an end.

That night, Woody went to Crow's place, and when I went to retrieve him, she asked to take a walk. We passed by the devil dog, who threw himself against his chain. Crow looked at the curtain-closed house with unease. She told me that the guy who lived there was stalking her and she had seen him slowly driving by her house many times. Once or twice, he had been skulking in the nearby woods.

"Shouldn't you tell the cops?" I asked.

"Oh, they wouldn't help out," she said. "The guy's father is a judge in town. They'd just tell me that I was exaggerating." A surprising instinct to protect Crow once again arose in me.

The woods along the road contained the usual Southeast Alaska mix of cedar, hemlock, and spruce, with blackberry bushes reaching across the ditches. Crow began pointing out subtle gradations of color between the trees, naming off shades of green: viridian, lime, apple, moss, olive, and emerald. She saw shapes in the trees: bodies, faces, and sometimes animals. She perceived the forest as an artist sees the forest, a world of detail, form, and impressions.

"I'm afraid I'm not cut out to be a painter," I said. "Never graduated past stick figures."

"I can teach you to draw," she said.

"No way, it's beyond me."

She laughed. "I know I'm clumsy and a bit thick in the head, but I can draw and can teach you," she prodded. "It's a matter of learning shapes and combining them, that's all."

"I can see it now. Me, Carrie, and Rachel on the floor with our coloring books."

"Oh, they wouldn't mind. Might even lend you their crayons if you're lucky."

Our arms touched. A subtle electricity passed through me. When we ambled back home, the devil dog lunged against his chain a couple more times. Woody strutted proudly down the street, making sure he noticed.

Over the next few weeks, Crow and I started to hang out every day as a fondness of her and the two girls grew. On one rare night, with a billion stars out, Crow and I climbed up on the roof of Hooverville. Woody stayed up at her place, playing fetch with a stuffed dinosaur that Rachel kept throwing across the room for him.

Pegasus, Cassiopeia, and the Big Dipper were shining. Lying there in the dark on some blankets, feeling Crow and the stars close, we fell into a kiss without stopping to think what it meant. It had been a long stretch without any intimate touch for me. My body was starved for contact. It just felt right and warm in the night air, surprising and easy to roll around with Crow. And while the heavens turned and shooting stars burned through the atmosphere, we loved there on the roof beneath it all.

Chapter 23

A CLAN HOUSE

January 1987

The elders told me that Saxman needed a clan house, modeled after a traditional one, where the dancers could perform, where the elders could gather and potlatches happen. I wondered if some of the old-growth trees Cape Fox was downing for the Japanese could be used to build it—a nobler end for them, seemed to me.

Steve Reeve, lands planner for Cape Fox, was a proactive and visionary fellow who began to create some sketches of what the tribal house could look like. We considered the village area. Currently, there was a large community hall, a couple dozen deteriorating totem poles, and a shack made of boards and discarded building materials where Nathan Jackson worked, one of the most renowned carvers in the nation. We outlined a rough plan for a simple theater in the community hall, a new carving center, the tribal house, and a village store that could sell traditional things made by hand in Saxman.

All of this had to be done on unpaid overtime. Soon, twelve-hour days became the norm. The new CEO at Cape Fox, Craig Burger, was a young guy of thirty, with a background in finance. Smart and self-effacing, he put Native shareholders' interests first in working to stabilize the corporation. He also supported my nascent tourism efforts.

Soon, my work life included attending numerous gatherings at Delores's house, City of Saxman council meetings, and a half dozen other Native organizations. Though Saxman only had a population just north of 350, you couldn't throw a stick without hitting a political organization. There were camps of the Alaska Native Brotherhood and Alaska Native Sisterhood, a chapter of a local Indian Reorganization Act, a local chapter of Tlingit and Haida Indian Tribes of Alaska, and a few others. All of them had opinions about what a cultural tourism village might look like; most were noncommittal and suspicious.

By and large, the people in Saxman wanted to wait and see if the plan succeeded before they came on board. In the aftermath of the fiasco with Dave Sisewell—still an open wound in the community—no one was about to jump onto another white guy's scheme. Little development had occurred in Saxman since the Civilian Conservation Corps had moved the totem poles to the park in the 1930s. Who was this young outsider talking about tribal houses and carving sheds and moving things around? Sisewell's projects had been mostly out of sight; only a handful of shareholders had ever visited the logging or sawmill or failed hotel project. But this development was just down the street in the middle of Saxman.

One unlikely ally was the cowboy-hat-wearing mayor of Saxman, George Wilson. George was a bit of an outsider himself, a Tlingit, but not a member of the three principal families that controlled Saxman political life. He got elected as mayor because the job had chewed up most everyone else. George was a bit blustery but had a no-nonsense, get-it-done style that seemed to work, despite the rumblings behind his back.

"It's a thankless job," he confessed as we stood in the totem park. "You know Indian people, they smile and laugh with you but can be pretty mean when they mean to." A toothpick bounced along his lips. "You heard the story of the crab pot, haven't you?"

He didn't wait for my response. "When one crab is just about to make it to the top to get out, the others reach up to pull him back down. That's a crab pot full of Indians."

The politics among the three main Saxman families was intense. If someone rose up as a leader, he or she faced enormous pressure. The three families were like partisan parties— Democrats, Republicans, and Independents. Then there were the "outsiders" who lived in Saxman, white, mixed race, Haida or Tongass Tribe Tlingits, who did not fit in and were largely tolerated but ignored. Every job filled or opportunity given was registered by the Saxman body politic. It was the Strongs against the Teweys against a rogue group, the Wishnells. Though comprising only 10 percent of the village population, the Wishnells never broke step and voted together as a bloc, whereas the two big families often split into factions.

In public, Saxman presented itself as one large family, but privately there was little trust. Some feuds had lasted decades. Behind closed doors, Delores spoke against Amy Tewey, who, in turn, claimed Delores was the root of all the problems and controlled everyone else and so on and so on. The biggest question was, Which family would benefit most from the tourism project?

The mayor was willing to get behind my idea, though. The project offered a significant annual contract that Cape Fox would pay to the city to run the tour and, in addition, Saxman would get a new tribal house, restored totems, new buildings, and a bunch of jobs.

"You keep working on it, young fella," George told me. "I'll get the council behind it."

We had made it through the previous summer at the Frontier Saloon, but just barely. Delores told me years later that she never got over the shame of it, performing in a saloon with her kids. But the tour companies at least knew who we were now. They were impressed enough to listen to a new idea— an idea to take cruise passengers by bus out to Saxman. We now faced a big problem. A small group of dancers and a few decaying totem poles were not enough to sustain a successful tour experience. The tribal house was at least a year away from being built. We had to create something else in the meantime.

Chapter 24

WHITE RAVEN

May 1987

The dancer, bare-chested under a mountain-goat blanket, raised his head and cawed loudly like a raven. His powerful thighs pounded moccasins on the cedar-planked floor in time to drumbeats. Deer hooves clacked on his ankles, and delicate eagle down fell from his headdress through the forested light.

Chris Makua, whose Tlingit name was Koocheesh, was half Tlingit, half Hawaiian, and a resident of Saxman. Tall, wiry, and strong, he was a gifted dancer performing in the Saxman Community Hall in front of 150 tourists. He was a member of a Tlingit theater troupe, Naa Kahidi, the centerpiece of our new tour.

Chris had come to Saxman as a stranger, but had rediscovered his ancestry there. Years before, while serving time in a California prison, Chris was jumped by rival gang members, his throat slit, and left for dead. He recovered, but the attack left him with a permanent, scratchy, thin falsetto that rose in pitch the more passionately he spoke. After release, Chris embarked on a spiritual quest in the desert. There, he had a vision of a forest-covered mountain that, later, traveling in Alaska, he recognized as Deer Mountain above Saxman. He discovered that this mother had been a member of the Bear (Teikweidee) Clan of the Tongass (Taantakwaan) Tribe.

Naa Kahidi and Chris were performing on a set in the red community hall built to resemble an old tribal house. It was the first day of our cultural heritage tours. All the cruise lines passed on the offering, except Princess Tours, who was willing to take a gamble on it.

Naa Kahidi brought to life a Tlingit creation myth, *Raven and the Box of Daylight*, written and directed by Dave Hunsaker. It told of a time when the world swirled with darkness.

Inside a clan house, a chief kept special treasures locked in a cedar box. One day, by firelight, Raven saw the shiny treasures in the box and wanted them for himself. He turned himself into a spruce needle and dropped into a stream that floated into the drinking cup of the chief's daughter. She swallowed it and later became pregnant.

A beautiful and willful boy grew to be the apple of his grandfather's eye. The boy had one overriding fascination in life, though: to see inside of the *special box*. The chief told him he could have anything but *that*, so the boy cried and cried. Finally, his grandfather relented, and the boy ran over and opened the box. The first stars in the world leapt out and rose through the smoke hole to be scattered in the night sky!

Grandfather said that was enough and refused to let his grandson open the box again. But a short time later, the boy opened the box on his own when the chief was outside, and the moon shot up through the smoke hole! The old man was very angry. Still, the boy wanted to open the box a third time and cried. Nothing could console him. The chief couldn't stay mad at his grandson for long, however. He sighed and let him open it again, and out shot the sun, up through the smoke hole, to illuminate the world!

As soon as it did, the little boy turned himself back into Raven, cawed loudly, and flew up toward the smoke hole. But he got stuck there, and that is how Raven, who was originally a white bird, turned black from the soot and has been black ever since.

The show was a big success with the tourists. A teenage tour guide then took them into the totem park and told stories of the poles. In the nearby carving shed, they watched Nathan Jackson carving Saxman's first totem poles in fifty years.

Things were not so smooth with the Strongs, however. Delores didn't like it one bit that Naa Kahidi was performing for tourists instead of the dancers. To ask her to sit out the first summer was a big deal for her. Delores trusted me, but I was also wary of her family's political capriciousness. She was the true authority in the village; everyone knew it. As the matriarch of the largest family, if she didn't go along with something, it didn't happen.

The Strongs were benefiting more than any other Saxman family from the tourism experiment. Delores's son-in-law was the tour manager, and a half dozen other family members had jobs as well. The construction of the tribal house had begun in late summer, and all the planks were being hand-adzed by Saxman workers, some from the Strong family. Once complete, the tribal house would be a stage for the dancers, led by Delores.

But the Strong family began to grumble among themselves. They didn't like outsiders like Naa Kahidi in the village. Though two of the paid cast members were from Saxman, including Chris Makua, none were from the three main Saxman families that ruled village political life.

Delores called me over to her house. She sat in her chair in the living room wearing her beaded raven vest. She didn't offer me coffee or a place to sit.

"How come Sealaska is up there performing in our hall?" she said sharply. "We didn't ask them here." This wasn't an argument I was going to win.

"At the start of the summer," I said, "remember, I talked to you about how we needed something here in Saxman to bring the tour buses out? Until we can get the tribal house built?"

Delores was looking down. "Nobody asked me nothin'," she said.

Nobody asked me nothing was a common refrain in Saxman when things weren't going well. It was a way to opt out if matters started to go sour. The more important issue was pride. If things went sideways, how would it look? What would others say? If you offended Saxman's pride, you were done.

"It was my family that kept this goin'!" she said with a raised voice. She pointed up the hill toward the totem park. "The dancers. Where are they in all this?"

"That's coming," I said with a slight shake in my voice. "That's why we're building the tribal house."

Asking her to trust me, a white outsider, was ludicrous. The ghost of Dave Sisewell's betrayal was still ever present in Saxman. Since he had been kicked out, Cape Fox had had to retrench to survive. The tourism operation was the first new endeavor since his departure.

"Why aren't the dancers up there?" she asked empathically.

What could I say? The truth was that, on their own, the dancers were not enough of a draw to get people to pay twenty-four dollars and hop on a bus to Saxman to see them perform in a gymnasium. We were dealing with corporate tour companies who were selling a shore excursion competing with helicopter trips, whales, kayak adventures, and a force field of curio stores. Naa Kahidi was a world-class show tourists couldn't see anywhere else. Saying any of this to Delores, however, would be a death sentence.

"It's coming," I said. "The dancers will have their own place. The tribal house is going to be the centerpiece for you, for them. Meanwhile, Junior, Alex, Jimmy, Walter, Angel, and Katie all have jobs and more will be coming."

Delores was silent. Her head turned away, she muttered, "We don't get nothin'." My audience was over.

A number of weeks passed, and the Strongs demanded that Naa Kahidi leave the village. The cast and crew were unhappy as well. They were under a lot of stress, performing up to nine times a week. Naa Kahidi was putting on tremendous performances, doing superlative, authentic work in a tough situation. They poignantly felt Saxman's unwelcome.

Every day, a new challenge popped out of the box that would upset someone in some family. Moreover, Princess Cruises was breathing down my neck to make sure their passengers were getting their money's worth. The tribal house was going up, but very slowly. There were countless construction issues. For the tour, whenever buses arrived, we had to make sure that the totem carvers were present and that a teenager, working their first-ever job, showed up to lead the group of tourists around.

Just under the surface, lurked an uneasy peace. The tour company had issues with consistency, and the village had issues with being told what to do. But the two groups couldn't talk face to face. I had to dance in the liminal space of two cultures and diplomatically translate between them. If even a hint of a tour company complaint made it to the village, folks in Saxman would get deeply offended. From the company's standpoint, the tour was simply a product. To the people of Saxman, this was culture and pride.

Naa Kahidi felt unwanted; the Strong family wanted to revolt. Princess Tours was sending me written complaints about the tour, asking for more uniformity of experience, polish, and "on the clock" logistics. Meanwhile, the City of Saxman wanted more money, and the tour ultimately had to be a financial success for Cape Fox. Working six and seven days a week, at times sleeping under my desk, I could feel my feathers turning black from the smoke.

Our Hero

The Little Red Cabin

Woody on the front deck of the Little Red Cabin

In the doorway of the Little Red Cabin

Story time with Dr. Woody on the beach of the Little Red Cabin

Late afternoon Alaskan sun

Woody and Jake in the back of Trucka de la Ducka

With Jake, Woody, and Louie at Sweetwater Lake

Woody surveys Cape Fox road building operations

At the watering hole after a long day on the construction crew

The dog-creature from the black lagoon in the muskeg

Bringing down Cape Fox trees

A temple before the chainsaws

Interior of the tribal house during construction

Opening celebration of the Saxman Beaver House (photo: Hall Anderson)

Master carver Nathan Jackson in Saxman

Dr. Woody's Pet and Owner Look-Alike Contest, Blueberry Arts Festival
(photo: Hall Anderson)

Lillian of Parnassus

Shakri-La (photo: Bruce Schwartz)

Woody at low tide in Shakri-La's front yard

An expedition in the dogyak

Woody reclining for an art shot

Me and Woody on the back deck of The Palace

Woody crossing a frozen river

Woody's first fishing trip

Woody's favorite sleeping posture

Chew the Bone with Dr. Woody *at KRBD-FM*

Chapter 25

FALL OF THE MARLBORO MAN

October 1987

The morning's Cape Fox board meeting had proceeded uneventfully, yet a slight tension pervaded the room and people seemed to be avoiding each other's eyes. At lunch break, needing a breather from it all, I wandered around Saxman with Woody leading the way. The air was crisp with sea breeze and yellow-turning alders.

Woody was sauntering along, free-bodied, loose in his bones and minding his own business. Then, from across the street, a Rottweiler-shepherd blustered toward him. Woody's body stiffened, his gait slowed, and the hair along his spine stood on end, but he kept moving, a free dog just passing through. I had witnessed this a dozen times and prepared for the show.

Woody never started a dogfight. He was a bit like David Carradine's character in the TV show *Kung Fu*. Basically a peacekeeper, Kwai Chang Caine was often pressed into fighting to defend his life or another's from ill-intentioned thugs, who always ended up on the worse end of things.

An ill-intentioned thug-dog was approaching Woody now, who slowed to a wary readiness. The Rot sniffed Woody's butt with grave resolve. Each hair follicle of both dogs brimmed high. Woody subtly rotated his body and tried to keep walking on, unhurried but determined. *Just passin' through, dog.* The Rot, twenty pounds heavier and an inch taller, with an aggressive set of dark eyes and powerful jaws, thrust his shoulder into Woody's body and extended his nose over his back. I stepped away to watch, morbidly fascinated to see a master in action.

The air was thick and charged. The two engaged in a sophisticated alpha ritual, a complex choreography heightened by potential violence. Woody and the Rot were stiff as statues now, tails tall with strong, quick, almost-imperceptible twitches, until even those stilled to nothing. It was the calm before the storm. The Rot was angling for a provocation, but Woody would have none of it. Enraged by his stoicism, the Rot launched a blitzkrieg and went for the back of Woody's neck. The air erupted in maniacal, feral dog snarls.

Woody was rarely the biggest in a fight, as here, outweighed by twenty pounds, but he was the fastest—a bit like Sugar Ray Leonard in the ring. The Rot rose up, trying to gain traction on Woody's neck with his front legs, but Woody twisted, dipped, and rolled under him, then slipped above his attacker with frightening speed. With both his paws over the Rot's shoulder, he powered him down to the gravel and planted his teeth firmly in his neck. It was over in seconds.

And though flashing teeth and snarls went on for a few more rounds, the contest was over. There was a pause, and the Rot knew he was finished. He scrambled up, with a bloodstained neck, and trotted back to his yard with what dignity he could muster. Woody strutted a few steps, then walked on as he had before, the hair along his spine settling down. Seconds later, it all seemed forgotten.

I had tallied up a lifetime of conflict avoidance and had never been in a proper fistfight. Deeply admiring Woody's fighting style—to see him, an essentially peaceful dog, who knew how to take care of himself if attacked—was an inspiration to me.

Back at Cape Fox, unknown to me, another dogfight was about to unfold. Overlooking the forest from a second-story window, the boardroom sported a long rectangular wood table and fourteen chairs. At one end sat the chairman of the board, Albert Wilson, a tall, gentle, soft-spoken man who worked as a longshoreman. Next to him, the co-chair, Robert Strong, Delores's oldest. He had a nervous, infectious laugh and a big smile, but beneath it you sensed a land mine ready to go off.

At the far end sat the management team, President Ben David, the son of Jack David, the last truly admired leader in the village. Ben felt the shadow of his father's legacy. He carried a hidden frustration of never quite measuring up, never gaining the respect in the village his father had. Next to him sat the CEO, Craig Burger, around my age, in his white shirt and tie. I sat along the side, with the creek and the forest to my back.

David Goodenough, a consultant, was there as well. David had recommended that we hire Craig Burger following Sisewell's tenure. David had been brought in to help the management team deal with the intense stresses of the job. There was the normal strain to become a profitable company magnified tenfold by the pressures in the village for cash distributions and jobs. Add to those, issues of cultural sensitivity, Saxman politics, and the shadow of Sisewell's failures that had put the company on the brink. This was Goodenough's first day in Saxman. He sat on his own, away from the table at the end of the room.

As controller, I went over the financial statements while board members stared at the white pages of numbers, not belying any emotion. The picture was not good. The company's timberlands were barely vast enough to recover from nearly a decade of Sisewell's projects gone bad and the debt the company had taken on. So much had been lost, while white managers, accountants, bankers, logging companies, and lawyers had gotten paid.

Craig Burger, though, was a good guy and the right one to lead the rebound. A keen, analytical thinker, with good instincts and a sense of humor, who could keep his cool in a storm. Cape Fox was lucky to have him. But he was standing on shifting ground. The board had come to learn that Sisewell had also negotiated himself a bountiful severance package, including ten acres of their land. The shareholders, and particularly the Strongs, felt ripped off—and rightly so.

I then talked about the cultural tourism project, the tribal house, and the promising economic development in Saxman. Twenty-four Native employees were working, including ten teenagers. The totem park was being renovated, and a village store was planned as an outlet to sell local crafts. I paid special attention to mentioning the elders, how instrumental Delores was in all of it, and made a point of saying how the tribal house would be home to the dancers next year. The three members of the Strong family were looking down, unwilling to meet my eyes.

Craig Burger talked about the overall business operations. We had been shutting down money-losing operations—the sawmill that had gobbled up hundreds of thousands of dollars, a busted hotel development, a spending spree on logging equipment, a machinery supply company, and more. The logging operation had been cut to just a few employees. Craig emphasized the need to keep consolidating until things had stabilized financially.

"The worst thing," he warned, "would be to be forced into overharvesting precious timberlands during a down market."

Robert Strong suddenly blurted out loudly, "Mr. Chairman, how did this happen? How did we get in such a place? All this debt. I don't remember us agreeing to this." He stood up, pointing his finger at management, his voice rising in pitch. "We rely on you, the management team. What are we supposed to tell our shareholders?"

The president, Ben David, always trying to be conciliatory, said, "We've been through this, Robert. These were decisions that were made years ago—"

"Order, Mr. Chairman," Robert interrupted, "I have the floor."

Ben stood up and blew out a nervous breath, and his hands started to shake like orbital sanders. Ben was a shareholder and pretty well paid, so he was a target in the village. He suffered for it, though. He cared deeply and with all his heart, but Saxman was not kind to its leaders.

Robert Strong's pent-up emotion kept washing ashore in waves. "The elders, I think about the elders," he said passionately. "Those who fought for this corporation. We have to keep them in mind! They thought of us. What are we doing for our elders today?" He was choked by tears and spoke loudly. "I think about the ones who passed on! What would they say to you all?" he said, pointing at Craig and Ben and me. "I think of Jack David, Tillie Williams, Joe Wilson Senior."

There was a weighty silence in the room. Then, Ben David, his voice as taut as a high wire, yelled, "You're talking about my father!"

"Mr. Chairman, I have the floor," Robert interrupted again.

The chairman beat the gavel on the table. "Order," he called, "Robert has the floor."

Ben David paced the head of the room, his arms crossed over his chest. "Mr. Chairman, you tell me what am I supposed to say?" he blurted out. "We are working so hard!"

"Mr. Chairman . . . ," said Robert.

"Mr. Chairman," board member Florence Wishnell interrupted. "I make a motion for a ten-minute recess."

The chairman didn't seem to know what to do. "We have a motion on the floor," he said. "Do I hear a second?"

All of a sudden, sitting directly across from me, Willie Strong shot up out of his chair and shouted, "No one told us about any of this!" He was somewhere between rage and tears. "What about our elders!" And he pointed his finger at Ben and shouted louder: "You tell us, what do we say! They worked hard and what do they get for all of this?"

The chairman pounded his gavel repeatedly. "Order. Order," he said.

Ben David stormed out of the room.

"Thirty-minute recess," the chairman announced. The room slowly emptied out in silence.

I wandered over to David Goodenough, who had watched it all with interest.

"Well, that's a first day for you, huh?" I said jokingly.

David had a full head of snow-white hair and a large mustache. His eyes were kind, and he jiggled like a jelly roll when he laughed.

"Can I ask you something?" he asked.

"Shoot."

"Which of your parents was an alcoholic?"

This came out of left field. I was speechless, not sure what he was talking about.

"Um, I don't know . . . It wasn't that bad, really."

He smiled. "That's the second sign."

"What . . . ?"

"The second sign is you feel it wasn't that bad. That's what children of alcoholic parents do—when they become adults, they tell themselves it wasn't really that bad."

He spoke with a kind knowingness that made me pay attention.

"Okay, that's the second sign. What's the first?"

"The first sign was when that guy across from you started shouting, you disappeared. You left the room. I looked over, and it was like you were hovering two feet outside the window looking in."

I felt caught in a spotlight. He was right. At the moment Willie Strong had started yelling, I got very still. That was my usual approach to emotional outbursts, safer out of the fray, yet my stomach had been paralyzed into knots.

"Um, yeah. It was my dad," I admitted. "I'll give you beginner's luck on that one, but it didn't affect me that much. He was a social drinker, really, not abusive or anything."

David laughed kindly again. "So that's sign number three. That you believe it didn't affect you that much."

Who was this guy? If he hadn't so deftly infiltrated my defenses, I would have walked right out of the room.

On the drive back to Hooverville, David's comments haunted me. It took me back to a forgotten drive in Boxtown years before. During an audit of an oil refinery in Tacoma, a secretary came in and told me I had a call. It was my mom.

"Wardy," she said, her voice cracking. "It's your father . . . He's here." And then she started to cry. Dad had been missing for a week, on a long binge or hiding out. Over the past year, he had become more remote and subject to depressions. He'd often disappear, but when he came back, it was never talked about. Everyone pretended it hadn't happened.

Over the previous six months, my mom and I had been taking a class at an alcoholic detox center to teach us to confront

Dad's alcoholism. It was a disease, we were told, and we couldn't rescue him. We had to wait until he hit rock bottom. Meanwhile, they advised us that the morning after a drinking binge, we were to communicate to Dad how his drinking affected us, how it made us feel. And we had to do this not just once, but repeatedly. We weren't to try and change him, they told us, but instead just let him know how it affected us.

It was scary stuff. "Dad," I'd say, my voice wavering, "when you came home drunk last night, it scared me."

He'd hang his head and say with a twist of guilt, "Well, I guess I've been a *horrible* father, haven't I?"

My mom would chime in. "Oh, Doug . . . ," she'd say, pregnant with shame. He'd walk out of the room, and she'd run to the bedroom and shut herself in. The house would hum with an impenetrable silence. Hours later, Mom would emerge from her room, come into the kitchen, and start making dinner. Dad would be reading the newspaper. Nothing more was ever said about it.

On the drive home from Tacoma, the tension of twenty-three years broke, and tears poured down my face, blurring my eyes. Tears for having to be the strong one for my mom, tears for the fear of what was happening to my dad, tears for the frustration of not being able to fix it, and tears for a little boy who had felt all of his life he was the cause of it all—that something was wrong with him.

My dad's car in the driveway brought the accustomed chill to my midriff. I sat for a while before getting out and slowly walking in. The house was silent. And there in the living room stood my proud, proud father—broken. The Marlboro Man, in the middle of the room, shattered, his jeans ripped, his face red and puffy, looking hopelessly down at the ground. He couldn't take a step forward or backward.

He had been the go-to guy, the leader in any group, the engineer in Huntsville who had helped Wernher Von Braun design the Saturn V rocket that got us to the moon. The man with all the answers who was never wrong. The man, fishing in the rain, wearing only a T-shirt and shorts in forty-degree weather, kneeling down on the boat floor cutting bait or fixing an outboard motor with a chewed cigar in his mouth. The man who had raised four kids, built houses, helped me construct my first hydroplane, fixed generators, rewired cars. The guy who played Santa for Christmas, who had been *Big Bear* to me as a kid, getting down on his hands and knees so I could put a pillowcase over his head and ride him around while he growled.

He had done his best to be a good father. But his love was deeply limited, unable to express it or to admit pain or know what to do with it. Pain to him was failure. *All emotion should be suppressed.* Keep the mask on—that's how he was raised.

"Get his bag," I said to my mom. The detox hospital had prepared us for this, to have a small suitcase of his things packed and ready. I went up to him, frightened that he might explode in anger. But standing next to him, the level of his defeat was apparent. He couldn't raise his head or look at me.

"Dad," I said. "We're going to take you somewhere you can get some help."

And this strong, strong man, who never asked anyone for a hand or would let anyone tell him what to do, let me take him by the elbow and lead him out to the car.

Chapter 26

DARKNESS IN HOOVERVILLE

Spring 1988

We made it through the first year of tourism in Saxman, while, in Hooverville, life was getting a bit odd. One day, Woody led me up to Crow's place. She was there with Michael, a sweet guy from Ketchikan who was a folk singer. After Michael left, Crow told me a secret that Michael was actually Rachel's father, but few people knew it. He had agreed to be a surrogate for Crow to have her second child. Michael had his own family and didn't seem to be the type to do that, but I accepted it as strange but true.

The next day, she, Woody, and I went for an adventure in my fourteen-foot skiff, up George Inlet to a special lagoon. We hummed along into the fine-grained day. Woody's nose to the sky, a lazy, dreamy look on his face. We passed through a bottleneck inlet, crossed a teardrop bay, and bumped ashore at a sandy beach. New blueberries and huckleberries were just appearing on the vine, not yet sun-sweetened for the black bears crawling out of their winter dens.

Up a grassy knoll above the cove, we laid out a blanket. The sun warmed my skin, and her body felt good close. But as usual, I felt slightly uneasy, off-kilter, around Crow. It was hard to put my finger on it, but she had a way of getting under my skin.

"This is divine here," I said.

She sighed. "Excepting that I'm here, I suppose," she said, fishing for an objection.

"I like you here," I said. But I didn't mean it. I wanted a break from everything: from Crow, Hooverville, and Saxman, a way back to a simpler existence with Woody like we had at the Little Red Cabin.

My eyes closed, the sun seeped into my body, the blue sky and a light breeze off the water intoxicating. She reached over and one thing led to another—eventually a bout of anxiety-fueled sex settled things for a while. We lay apart afterward, each in our own world.

"I suppose you'll be leaving me up and soon, huh?" Crow said, breaking the silence.

I didn't want to get into it with her. "What are you talking about?" I asked half-heartedly.

"You're just using me, you know."

"What the . . ."

She sat up. "I'm just a piece of meat to you."

"Crow, what are you doing?" I asked, irritated. "No, I care about you . . . you're amazing," I added as I looked away, trying to reassure both of us.

"I know I'm a bit slow and backwoods like, not a polished stone. I'm rough around the edges, not your type."

"What's my type?"

"Black-haired, easygoing, a quiet Taoist woman."

I lay awhile on edge not sure what to say, before getting up and walking away. That always made me feel safer, to go be alone.

Woody and I wandered off and explored the shore and tidelands. Late in the day, we all climbed into the skiff and zipped back to Hooverville, glad for the engine that covered up any impulse to talk.

Back home before I left her for the night, she told me that the guy next door, who owned the devil dog, had been stalking her again. She said he was outside her house in the woods sneaking around the night before. This had the usual desired effect: to awaken in me a wave of protective energy toward her and the two girls.

Woody and I took a twilight walk to the end of the road and made our way past the devil dog's place. Blankets were drawn over all the windows, and in the driveway stood a jacked-up black pickup covered in mud. The devil dog stared at us darkly. Woody assumed his usual prance, taller in his legs, alert but aloof, hoofing along, daring his adversary to charge.

The devil dog took his accustomed silent run to the end of his chain. The pure ferocity of this ritual was always frightening and morbidly fascinating to me, watching him collar himself at the end of his chain. But something went wrong this time. The chain snapped as if it were a string, unleashing months of pent-up rage. Like a black locomotive that had jumped its tracks, the devil roared straight for Woody, pure hatred pouring from its eyes.

Woody moved over and, though outweighed by forty pounds, lunged to meet him head-on. It was no contest. The mad dog crashed into Woody from uphill and smashed him handily into the ditch, pressing him into the mud and flashing his teeth above his neck, ready to kill.

In that moment, something rose up inside of me, a roar from my gut, feral and fierce. I jumped down into the ditch to tear out his throat with my bare hands. But my yell had done the trick. As if hit by a shock wave, the devil jumped off Woody and trotted back to his place in the yard. Woody climbed up, half his face covered in mud. He shook, posturing, unwilling to give the devil an inch. But in Woody's eyes was a look of fear I had never seen before. The best dogfighter I ever knew had, for the first time, met a force that could kill him.

The devil stood in his yard, looking at us like a malevolent king. I took a step toward him and said in a venomous tone that rolled from the root of my being, dark and low, "You keep the *fuck* away!" I knew in that moment, if needed to, I, too, could kill. And he knew it as well. He looked me in the eye and slid silently away, behind the house.

Chapter 27

OVER THE EDGE

May 1988

A desperately needed break from Crow, Saxman, and Hooverville turned out to be just up the road: KRBD, the local community radio station. The internet did not yet exist, and in Alaska, community radio was a lifeline on dark, rain-socked nights. A lot of folks went without TV, and for many, the radio was the only voice they heard at night.

I was now a regular DJ on Saturday nights, a rock 'n' roll show called *Over the Edge*. Woody was in the studio along with my fellow partner in crime and rebel, Martini. Making radio was the most profound expression of democracy imaginable. It gave me a laboratory to express myself and to make some art, a foreign concept in my family. KRBD gave us the freedom to play and say what we wanted, sending original sounds out via the "theater of the mind" to remote bays, vessels, and cabins.

Woody, too, had joined the fun. It was 7:30, time for another episode of *Chew the Bone with Dr. Woody*. Woody had become the town's cosmic dog psychologist, answering the problems of troubled pets or the two-leggeds who lived with them. It was a crazy idea, an experiment to let off some steam. People wrote to him via the station. I was Spot, his on-air voice, and channeled answers from Dr. Woody's inexhaustible well of dog wisdom. He spoke in a fractured German accent, sounding a bit like Dr. Ruth.

> *Dear Dr. Woody,*
> *Our dog Snuff, a coonhound, has insomnia. He stays awake most of the night, clumping around the house moaning and sighing. Can you help us?*
> *—Wendy Foster*

> *My dear Wendy,*
> *I spoke with Snuff. You know that party two weeks ago? The one when everyone got so loaded and passed out? Well, I have some unfortunate news for you. You left the TV on all night, and Snuff had nothing better to do than to watch. Late in the night when the dark and rain were at their worst, a rerun of* The Exorcist *came on, and Snuff, wide-eyed and alone, surrounded by plastered, passed-out humans, watched as Linda Blair's head twirled around and green vomit spewed from her mouth.*
> *Wendy . . . Snuff is haunted. In fact, he might be possessed.*
> *There is only one cure. You must dress up as a priest and run into the living room when Snuff does not expect it, brandishing a cross in front of you, and yell, "Get thee behind me, Satan! You will leave my dog now!" And when Snuff's*

head starts spinning around, you must grab his
snout and cram a Big Dad Beef Stick down his
muzzle. This should take care of the bad spirit
for now. You must then feed him a Big Dad Beef
Stick once a day for forty days. And make the
cat sleep outside. Then Snuff will be free.
     Okay, Be kind . . . Be Dog . . . You're welcome,
—Dr. Woody

Martini had been laughing into her cupped hands as Dr.
Woody was on the air. As a song played, she let out a chuckle,
bouncing up and down in her chair across the console from
me. Martini was a cylindrically built Taurus with pale skin
and a magnificently expressive mug. She had a puppet face that
went through such a multitude of dramatic facial offerings as
she talked, you'd look above her for the strings. Laughing, her
whole body rocked with sharp jiggles, her eyes squeezed shut
and tearing up.

She had one fashion scheme: black-widow-spider décor—
with an occasional dash of red. Her hair was black and so was
every piece of clothing she owned. Martini worked at the Forest
Service as a draftsman, trying to hang on until retirement. She
created detailed drawings for bridges, logging roads, or remote
camps. A field engineer said once when he saw her working on
sketches for a camp, "Martini's doing the drawings! Oh God, I
can see it now. All the outhouses will be black with little lines
of red trim!"

The phone rang. It was someone who lived on Pennock
Island.

"Hi," he said. "Hey, our son Jacob has been listening and
just said his first three-word sentence. You know what they
were?"

"What?" I asked.

"Woody . . . the . . . Dog."

The most famous dog psychologist in town was sacked out on his side in the adjoining record room, where LPs were stacked floor to ceiling, organized by blues, jazz, classical, R and B, country, folk, show tunes, spoken word, and rock 'n' roll. During a week on KRBD, you could tune in and hear every genre of music with a local at the controls.

Over the Edge became my once-a-week, moment-to-moment expressive theater and introduction to a way of life where creativity, not spreadsheets, were central to my existence.

Radio was an intimate art form. Everyone listening traveled to his or her own private mindscape. We would get call-ins from Quonset huts in remote bays, cabins deep in forests, fishing boats in Clarence Strait, or the swing shift at the LP mill.

I spun a Richard and Linda Thompson tune, "Shoot Out the Lights," which prompted Martini to shout, "I got one!" She hopped into the record room to grab Bonnie Raitt's "Give It Up or Let Me Go" and cued it up just as "Shoot Out the Lights" ended.

"Bonnie!" Martini said with deep reverence. "She knows what she wants." Martini danced in her chair with headphones on. "Bonnie can stand on her own with any slide player in the world," she said with a professional stoner's authority. "Triple Scorpio," she added. Sitting back, she said, "I'd die for that head of hair."

Dr. Woody came over to play *Ewok toss* with Martini. In his snout, he held out a little stuffed Ewok she had given him. Martini threw it through the door into the record room, and he raced around the equipment to bring it back, which he would do a hundred times.

As Martini's record wound down, I cued up a Tom Waits song. But then I was struck with an inspiration, a song that summed up my relationship with Crow. There were just twenty seconds left of Bonnie when I thought about how Bob

Dylan's "Tangled Up in Blue" would fit perfectly. I burst out of the chair and pulled myself around the corner into the record room, made the fifteen feet across to the records along the wall, and rifled through the Dylan LPs. Bonnie now had ten seconds to go.

I sprinted back into the air room, slipping the record out of its jacket on the move, flipped it to side one, pulled Tom Waits off turntable one, and with the other hand, laid Bob on the platter. As Bonnie bit into her last note on turntable two, I back-spun "Tangled Up in Blue," hit the Play button, and pushed the slider up. The first note of Bob segued perfectly and hit the airwaves as if it had been planned that way an hour ago. Out in the fjord, in cabins and in cells at the Ketchikan City Jail, people listened, unaware of the acrobatics that had taken place behind the mic. It sounded good, smooth as fine wine, while Martini whooped and yelled, "Good one!"

The phone rang. *"Over the Edge,"* I said.

It was a purse seiner, *Night Rider,* calling in on the ship-to-shore radio. "Hey!" a loud, thin voice yelled back. There was partying in the background. "We're anchored here in Helm Bay and just wanted to let you know, we're digging it!"

Over the Edge was on its way to our first Listener's Choice Award, given by KRBD'S audience. It was a kick to us because all we did was have fun and thumb our noses at the establishment. My teenage anger that had been suppressed inside a three-piece suit began to emerge. The more I thought about my parents, my schooling, and the whole mess of my culture, the more I felt a burning inside, to jab a finger at Boxtown or any authority figure—especially older male ones—as well as any force destructive to nature. Anger at my government, anger at myself for the masquerade I had lived, anger at the irony of working for a logging company. Anger at everything. Rock 'n' roll was the perfect loudspeaker for that rage.

Inside the warm, incandescent glow of the studio, we improvised our way through a set featuring ringing guitars (the Byrds, Jerry Garcia, George Harrison); another set we called story songs (Ramblin' Jack Elliott, the Kinks, Rita Coolidge); and, one of my favorites, a set of angry songs (John Lennon, Patti Smith, and others) that always got a good response, especially from the guys working the night shift at the mill.

After *Over the Edge* had broadcast its sonic anarchy across the archipelago night, Woody and I stepped outside the studio in the dark to the rush of Ketchikan Creek tumbling by. It was the same creek that met miners in the 1890s, fishermen in the 1920s, and prostitutes and drunks looking for respite from a rain-drenched, lousy life. Along the side of its endless rush, the Tongass people had caught fish and picked berries. The sound of the creek rode down the mountain like a landslide before any human walked the earth. It carried the deep rumblings of large mammal bellies, the spawn of salmon, and the breaking of the first seedpods of the ancient trees.

Woody and I hopped into our new truck, a 1981 Ford F-250 with a camper on the back I called The Palace. We rambled on out toward Hooverville, but kept driving, listening to the tape of *Over the Edge*. The Palace carried us to the bullet-hole-pocked *End* sign at the southern edge of town, and stopped in the middle of the gravel road facing the dark forest.

I switched off the headlights, opened both doors, and turned up our radio show. Woody jumped up on the tailgate as I cracked a beer, and we watched the late-night stars together. Dr. Woody stood, then turned around, dropped his bones on the tailgate, sighed once, and fell asleep.

He lay curled up beside me, in a lone pickup in the middle of the dark, the trees sharp-topped and dense against the night, with the Marshall Tucker Band playing. My hand rested on his back as he breathed slow and steady, bringing a deep calm to my soul. It was all I needed, really: a beer, music, the forest, and Woody.

Chapter 28

SAXMAN CULTURAL VILLAGE

Summer 1988

The crown jewel of Saxman's cultural renewal, a traditional cedar-planked tribal house, shone like a new sun behind the totem park. It was a long, rectangular building, fifty by eighty feet, with two ninety-foot spruce trees spanning the interior to support the roof. Every surface inside and out had been hand-scalloped with adzes by a small army of Saxman workers. A totemic beaver design fronted the house, carved by Nathan Jackson, who had also created four beautiful beaver house posts that held up the spruce beams.

While the house had been under construction, I often had climbed up to sit on the roof beams and gaze down the hill to the Tongass Narrows, blue-black in the fading twilight, while in the foreground, haunted silhouettes of totem poles emerged from the trees. To see a totem pole from behind at dusk within the outlines of evergreens is to catch a glimpse of the mystical and shamanic nature of Southeast Alaska—a land surrounded by luminous and dark waters, where animals are a daily, powerful presence; where the spirit of the primeval hides; where people once spoke to the animals and the animals spoke back.

The house stood now, complete, a place of resonance, beauty, and honor, its roofline mirroring the lines of the mountains behind. Our second tour season was upon us. Visitors found something hard to find in Alaska: a one-on-one experience with Native people in their own community. Nathan Jackson, one of the great carvers on the coast, was a highlight, as was the commanding but gentle figure of Delores and her dancers, especially the grandchildren, some just three or four years old in their tiny button blankets dancing in the tribal house. Women elders sat at workbenches sewing beads on moose hide, making vests, or crafting cedar baskets.

Teenagers led groups of non-Native people around to tell them stories of the totems. The new village store was providing a unique source of income as tourists bought beaded moccasins, vests, drums, masks, and other regalia made by local women.

In the park, a group of tourists in their plastic rain slickers were flocking around Richard, one of the tour hosts. He was describing the design on his vest.

"It's a raven. See its straight beak? That's how you tell," he said. "An eagle has a curved beak. Raven's my grandmother's clan."

A gray-haired lady asked him about his plans.

"I want to go to college," he said proudly, surprised that anyone would even care to ask him. "Like to work construction management," he added.

Richard had always been in trouble, suspended from school, caught up in drugs and truancy. Nearby, a girl named Lucy was confidently telling another group surrounding her about the Abe Lincoln pole. Hired six months ago, at the time,

Lucy had been so shy, she looked down at the tops of her shoes when spoken to.

To have people interested in them and respecting them was an epiphany. That was not a message Native kids often received in the rain-slicked back streets of Ketchikan.

There continued to be growing pains. Though the tour company offered "Saxman Cultural Village" as a shore excursion, the Saxman people did not see themselves as a product. They wanted respect and flexibility around too many hard-and-fast rules and schedules. I sensed their vulnerability as the first village in Southeast Alaska to open itself to visitors in this way. Things had happened fast. What had begun as a cultural program was becoming more and more a business.

The industrial-tour world cared about numbers, money, and consistency of customer experience. Yet we had built the village around the idea of an *inner circle*, inside of which the clan members would stay as truthful as possible to the culture, doing what they would do to teach the young and to support cultural activities such as storytelling, dance, artwork, and totem carving. Tourists were invited to look in on these activities.

It was a model that asked for tolerance to account for changing circumstances and personnel. If elders did not want to or could not come to the tribal house on a given day, what were we to do? Fire them? The dancers were sixty strong, but as few as a dozen might show up for a performance. We hired coordinators who were rock solid, such as Junior DeWitt and a young Saxman guy, Steve Williams, both of whom were real good at improvising. We also hired many more teenagers than we needed for tour hosts. On any given morning, when a cruise ship came into view in the Narrows, we scrambled to assemble a team for that day. Scheduling things more than a few days in advance didn't work. Every day, a new crisis rose up. It was a near-impossible circus to manage. Most days, it felt like backing a trailer down a narrow boat ramp with failing brakes and nothing but the side mirror to steer by.

Chapter 29

MRS. CUSTER

Summer 1988

The phone rang in my office overlooking the creek. A Native kid from the village yelled in a high-pitched voice, "It's Woody! He's *humping*!" and hung up.

Sure enough, the back door of the office was open, and Woody was nowhere in sight. Taking off had become almost a weekly event with him. It was a mystery where he went in Saxman, but he always came back—eventually.

I walked across the parking lot, through a scrub-brush clearing where abandoned vehicles and busted machinery rusted away amid the weeds, and proceeded down Killer Whale Avenue looking for Woody. There was a big potlatch the coming weekend, and folks were getting ready. Kids were playing in front of one of the houses, and a lot of people were heading to the backyard.

And there in the middle of a circle of folks, Woody the Dog was stuck in an erotic coupling with a white mutt they called

Mrs. Custer. She had trapped him hard and fast between her haunches.

"Hey, amigo," I said. "What kind of trouble you got yourself in, eh, *vato*?" Woody looked at me sheepishly, embarrassed.

"Is that *your* dog?" a little girl asked.

"Hey, Ward, you should teach your dog some manners." It was Willie, Delores's youngest. Everyone in the circle laughed.

"Nah," I said, "I think he learned this on his own."

"Well, maybe you should take some lessons from him. Help you find a wife?" Another round of laughter.

Something had to end this profound insult to Woody's noble soul. I filled a bucket with water, walked over, and tossed it over the two dogs, hoping it would shock Mrs. Custer to let loose her vise grip. Instead, two sopping, still-coupled, sad-looking dogs maintained their impasse. But worse, the shock of the water had turned Woody around, and now he stood butt to butt with Mrs. Custer, as stuck inside her as the totem boy in the park with his hand trapped in the oyster.

Nothing to do but wait it out. Junior DeWitt came up and looked on for a while and laughed along with everyone else.

"You coming to the potlatch?" he asked.

"Yeah, I wouldn't miss it," I said.

"You still got that Gregor of yours?"

"Yeah, I do. Runs pretty good, too."

"How about you and I go out Saturday morning. Fish for some halibut. Bring back a big one for the potlatch."

A cheer went up. Mrs. Custer had finally relented, and Woody wriggled himself free and stumbled over, head down and shell-shocked.

"Yeah," I said. "Yeah, sure."

"Pick me up four a.m.," he said. To Woody, he scolded, "Hey, white dog, that's what you get for messin' around with Injuns," and went off howling with laughter, repeating what he said to others, who echoed his laugh.

On the way back, we stopped in at Delores's. The Saxman folks really didn't understand my relationship with Woody. To most of them, dogs were just animals, cute when puppies, mostly left to fend for themselves outdoors, some free roaming, a lot of them tied up. But to have a dog always with you, that rode in your car, that had a radio show, that you talked to in Spanish . . . well, it was a bit much.

Woody had had enough adventure for one day. He lay down on Delores's porch and watched the cars below zing by on Tongass Highway. I knocked. Someone looked through the curtains. It took a while before the door opened. Inside, a big group of Delores's extended family was there, getting ready for the potlatch, including five sisters sitting around the kitchen table working on food and sewing.

"Oh, we heard about that dog of yours," said Chickie, a rotund sister with a smiling face and dark eyes. News traveled fast in the village. They called it the *Muskeg Telegraph*. If Woody wasn't famous before, he was now. There was lots of talk and lots of laughter in that house that day. I never heard as much laughter as at Delores's with a houseful of people. My culture seemed lonesome in comparison, isolated in fractured families that gathered at best in twos or threes or fours. On most Sundays at Delores's, thirty or more kids, parents, grandkids, and great-grandkids gathered.

Delores was at the kitchen sink, but acting strangely. She looked at me, then turned her back without a word. Lord knows what I had done now?

Chapter 30

OLD MAN HALIBUT

August 1988

We launched my fourteen-foot aluminum Gregor at Mountain Point, three miles south of Saxman. The dawn was crystalline with an indigo sky, and the sea was as soft as a down comforter. The air popped with salt. The Johnson sputtered up, and we cut our way toward the forested hillsides of George Inlet. Junior DeWitt rode up front, his stout body flattening the cushion. He wore a lined navy windbreaker zipped tight and a Sealaska cap over his black-slicked hair. A .22 rested in his lap—in case we saw any seals for the potlatch. Woody pointed his nose into the wind, toward the adventure.

The Gregor slipped through the buttery sea, scaring up a few seagulls. The pulp mill and Native corporations had yet to pock the hillsides with clear-cuts, and we looked upon the same as yet-unscarred forests that Junior's ancestors must have seen as they paddled across the strait in cedar canoes, hunting halibut with a big cedar hook and deer meat on a sharpened spike.

We raced past diving ducks, my hand trailing over the side of the boat, fingers slapped by the cold water. Junior pointed south, and I angled the skiff in the direction of the distant steep-faced hills—a palate of yellow cedar, hunter-green hemlock, and smoky-blue spruce. After a bit, we turned parallel to a nearly vertical wall of forested rock that rose hundreds of feet straight out of the water. Two ravens blew across the hemlock tops. A lone eagle sat on an old snag.

After traversing the shoreline awhile, Junior signaled for me to slow. I cut the engine. The wake rolled onto a tiny sliver of beach and spilled over rocks. Junior looked several times toward the hill, as if to get a bearing, toward where he said Old Man Halibut lived. After thirty more seconds of drift, he seemed satisfied and started to rig up two stalwart, stubby rods with big lead sinkers. He attached a wire leader to each to keep the line from tangling and speared frozen herring onto large hooks.

"Okay, let her drop," he said, handing me a pole.

Two ravens circled before hiding in the upper deck of an old cedar. The aluminum hull rocked gently as we slowly let our small cannonballs descend through the dark cold to rest two hundred feet in the cellar of George Inlet. It was so still, I could hear Junior breathe. With no other boat in sight, it seemed we floated on a newly born sea.

Junior talked about the potlatch. His sons had been up until three in the morning the past two nights getting the community hall ready and preparing food.

"One thing," he said, "at Indian doin's, you don't run out of food."

There would be potato salads and rice, salmon, seal grease, bear meat, ooligan oil, herring roe on kelp, fry bread, seaweed, and desserts. We'd bring in the halibut. We had hardly

gotten settled when my hook got snagged on the bottom. *Shit!*
I started to reel up. The pole bent almost to breaking. It was
embarrassing that so soon I might have to break the line and
lose the hardware.

"I snagged an old sleeping bag," I said.

My dad was a fisherman extraordinaire. Salmon were
his game. He'd come back with two or three big fish while
everyone else within two nautical miles got skunked. After
we moved from Alabama back to the Pacific Northwest, Dad
often took me as a teenager out fishing in Puget Sound. In his
nineteen-foot Sabrecraft, he dutifully intended to teach me
something about catching salmon. Invariably, though, I would
crawl down in the front of the boat and be asleep within an
hour of the poles in the water. He'd wake me up when he
hooked into a big one and let me reel it up.

The talents of fishing, like alcoholism, jumped a generation. Neither my dad's zest for scotch nor his skill in the fish
game were passed down to me. So this moment in George Inlet
made sense to me. It was inevitable that right away some huge
inanimate object would get tangled in my line.

After slowly coming up a few feet, the pole suddenly
dipped back down and tugged three times as if an elephant
had a hold of it. I couldn't believe the line didn't snap. And then
a distinctive laugh, Junior's cackle—*ho ho ho ho ho hooooooo.*
Then higher—*he he he heeeeeeee oh oh ohhhh!*—rolled out of
the boat and echoed off the rock walls.

"I don't think that's a sleeping bag," he said, and laughed
again.

A wrestling match ensued, trying not to let whatever was
down there pull me overboard. Junior reeled up his line, every
now and then letting off more giggles, before settling down in
the front of the boat, laying his head against the gunwale, and
pulling his hat partly over his eyes as if for a long nap.

"You go ahead," he said. "I'm just gonna sit back here and enjoy the fun."

"You bastard," I whispered between my teeth, which spawned another round of cackles, as I strained to lift the pole above my head. Woody watched it all, his head draped over the side, dreaming.

For the next forty-five minutes, a mid-boat tug-of-war with the underwater Goliath continued while Junior entertained himself at my expense. The muscles of my shoulders, biceps, and lower back ached from the clumsy ballet—arching the pole over my head and turning the reel three quick turns before the tip was pulled back down to the water's surface. Junior didn't waste a moment making the best of my struggle. I was a dartboard in a tavern helpless against his tosses. In a moment of supreme weakness, I asked him if he would spell me, that my arm muscles were about to fall off. His belly shook and loud hoots echoed down the bay, startling a flock of geese fifty yards away.

Sitting on the middle seat to rest, I leaned the pole against the side, but my overwhelming curiosity about what was on the other end of the line soon drove me to my feet again for the agonizing four or five feet a minute of upward progress.

Then, after what seemed an eternity, when every sinew and muscle in my body was complaining, the connector attached to the cannonball arose. We peered over the side into the crystal-green waters but couldn't see anything at first. Gradually, a wavering shape began to emerge. The water turned a deeper shade of green as the outline of what looked like a vampire in a large, dark cape appeared. I'm not sure if it was Junior or me who uttered, "Oh my God!"

This was why the Old Man had been so hard to pull up. He had arched his body and turned his spine concave to resist the upward pull. Minutes later, his head was only six inches from the surface. Exaggerations are expected in fish stories, but if Woody could talk, he would stand beside me to verify it. The fish was almost as long as our fourteen-foot boat. His eyes, bugged out atop his twisted face, were the size of eight balls. His mouth reflexively opened and closed, big enough to swallow a loaf of Wonder Bread in one gulp.

Junior joined in the mixture of giddiness and fear. My feet were braced against the boat's bottom ribs. The enormity of the halibut made me lose confidence about who would win if he became determined to yank me over into a slow, cold-green death. But my fears were displaced by the vision of our triumphant entry back to the village, heroes, hailed by everyone, asking us to tell our story over and over again.

A halibut is one of the most dangerous fish to land in a small boat. Stories abound of people who suffer broken legs or worse from the powerful thrashing of a large halibut thought to be long dead. People would shoot them in the water and believe it was all over only to have the Goliath wake up hours later and take out its vengeance on its would-be killers. Unless the bullet went through its brain, the size of a walnut, you couldn't kill a halibut. The fish had spent a lot of time on the bottom of the ocean, figuring out how to stay alive, and had done a pretty good job of it. The safest, most efficient thing to do is to stick it with a halibut harpoon or a shark hook to get a rope through its mouth. After it finishes thrashing, you draw it in and then hit it with a bat between the eyeballs. A lesser method is to use a gaff hook well secured to a rope, tied to the transom.

"Where's your gaff?" Junior said.

A pit opened in my belly. There it was, in my mind's eye, the gaff, leaning up next to my boat shed—twenty-one miles away.

"Shit," I muttered. Meanwhile the big eight-ball eyes kept looking at me, wondering who was going to make the next move. Junior looked around the boat for anything.

"Your gun," I said, "maybe you could shoot it."

Junior grabbed his .22 and climbed around to the back of the boat, but somehow, in a slumbering way, the pool-ball eyes registered movement, and almost as if he could read our intentions, he slid himself closer to the boat and hung so Junior would have to shoot straight down. We were in a small rocking boat, and Junior was not a small man. The chances he would shoot me or fall in were higher than the probability that he would hit the walnut in the center of our big friend's head. We both pondered what to do. My arms were almost locked in spasm, holding the pole high, not wanting to agitate the fish too much while we searched for another plan.

The halibut's steady gaze met mine in the clear water that separated us. As he looked at my strange, wavering shape above him, rather than fear, his eyes exuded a mixture of pain and perplexity. Despite his quandary, the main impression one got was of a quiet determination. He seemed confident of the outcome of our standoff.

Halibut are an undignified, kind of a crazy-looking fish, really, with twisted visage—eyes close together on top and a large crescent-moon mouth on the side. They are the great clown fish of the deep. How could you not laugh at a face like that? But as this giant's gaze continued to fix me, there arose the uncomfortable feeling that he could peer into my depths.

While one part of my mind was racing to find a solution to land this creature, another part was wrestling with a subtle kinship that had risen between him and me. I am a lousy fisherman, and he knew it, too. But I was not ready to give in.

"My toolbox!" I yelled to Junior. "Look in my toolbox!"

Junior popped it open and lifted up the tray of small tools. "For what?" he asked.

"I don't know," I said, looking the halibut in the eyeballs. "The hammer, grab the hammer."

Junior stood next to me with my claw hammer in his hand, looking at the fish, looking at the hammer, looking at me.

"What am I supposed to do with *this*?" he asked, bewildered. The ravens in the tree waited for my answer.

"Um," I said, "hit him with it."

Junior was about to laugh until he saw the level of anxiety coursing through me and realized my emotional well-being was teetering in the balance, clinging to a thread much less sturdy than the line holding me to the halibut.

"Hit him with it!" I yelled.

A few more hard-earned reels drew the old man's snout out of the water, so that his forehead was only inches below the surface. Junior held on to the boat's side, leaned over, and brought the hammer down hard onto the halibut's head, just behind his eyes, splashing water onto his arms and my face. The fish swiveled a bit in the water and seemed to blink. A new look came into his eyes: profound puzzlement.

"Hit him again!" I yelled. "Hit him again!"

And Junior did, but it seemed not to faze the fish at all.

I began to doubt the effectiveness of the hammer approach.

"Maybe you could thread a rope down his mouth and out his gill," I said.

This returned Junior to his mirthful self.

"*You*," he said, "can stick your hand in there if you want. I ain't sticking my hand down there!"

"Hit him again!" I screamed.

And he did. But this time as the hammer arced through the air, the edge of its claw caught the line.

It snapped.

In slow motion, the halibut began to slip away. Thoughts of jumping in to hold on to him careened into my mind. I was sick with the shock of the loss. Yet in the face of his undeniable descent to freedom, despite my despair, I hoped he was going to be okay. Maybe he'd have a gigantic headache for a while, but he deserved to live; he deserved to snooze on the bottom of the world and tell his grandchildren about the strange encounter he had with the barbarians from the surface. As he fell away into green darkness, he turned and gave the slightest kick of his tail goodbye.

For some time, Junior and I stared at the water.

"I don't feel very good," Junior said.

I couldn't utter a word. My sense of relief that the fish was going home was soon displaced by a profound sense of our defeat in the raw sunshine of midmorning. We would not be the heroes in the village today.

In the distance, other boats purred across the water. The ravens no longer talked in their trees. We would have been even poorer excuses for fishermen, though, if we didn't try again. We circled back above the same deep hole in the water. The rest of the morning, we didn't get a nibble. Even Junior's exhaustless humor fizzled as we tried repeatedly to get our minds off the Old Man. We settled into a long silence.

Then we decided on a pact. We wouldn't think about it anymore, and we wouldn't tell anyone. First of all, they would never believe us, but worse, we would have to relive our failure each time in the telling. Not talking about it or thinking about it would work, we figured. The Johnson fired up, and soon we were tumbling back toward Mountain Point. The air was fresh, and the wind braced my face. With all my might, I tried to forget the fish, tried to ignore the empty pit in the bottom of my stomach. Then, over the roar of the outboard, Junior's yell spread into the wind. "It's not workinggggggggggg!" All the way back, every few moments, he yelled the same refrain. "It's not workinggggggg!"

As we pulled into Mountain Point, another couple of guys were loading their boat into the water. "How'd ya do?" one of them asked.

Junior looked at him, then glanced at me.

"Nah, nothing," he said. "A nibble or two. That's all."

Chapter 31

GÁNYAA

August 1988

The potlatch was in full swing. Dance groups from villages all over Southeast Alaska had arrived to help christen the new tribal house. Tables were full of endless food, and the room resonant with long speeches in Tlingit and plenty of song and dance. Every kid, auntie, uncle, and family member from Saxman was there, helping in the organizing, the continuous food preparation, the serving or cleaning up. Included were the many people who, at home, talked derisively behind each other's backs, echoing family feuds older than anyone could remember. But here they were all together, sitting, laughing, sharing, dancing, forgetting all of that for a few hours.

The potlatch went on for three days and never lacked for food. All of Junior DeWitt's teenage kids were working in the kitchen. He and I laughed every time we saw each other, one of the other of us saying, *"It's not worrkinnnnng!"* But we kept our word and did not tell anyone about our fish story.

The Saxman hosts performed a long ceremony of gift sharing to the visiting families and clans from up the coast. The giveaways were impressive. They passed out stacks of Pendleton blankets, towels, gloves, hats, and other gifts liberally. A dance was performed for the local Salvation Army and a scholarship fund begun on the spot. Dozens of people danced up waving fives, tens, or twenties above their heads and dropped the bills onto a blanket spread on the floor—the way money should be shared in celebration, waved high and free and for the benefit of others.

It was time for the host group, the Cape Fox Dancers, to perform. Delores led them out, forty-five strong, from the two-year-olds to the aunties, young men and women, uncles, and grandparents. Their frequent performances for tourists over the last two summers had made them a force to contend with. Their welcome dance raised a mighty roar in the tribal house. So infectious were the drums and feet stomping on the cedar floor that people all over the hall rose out of their seats shouting and danced along.

At the end, the group turned their backs, clan crests proudly displayed. You could hear the heavy breathing in the hall, feel the sweat in the air and the reverence. The group then performed a canoe song, pantomiming the water journey with pointed dance paddles. Then came my favorite, the *Wild Man* dance. It was the story of a tribal member who is outcast and runs off to the woods in shame and there becomes a wild man, eschewing human companionship and company. But the women of the clan never lose hope in him, and the sisters coax him back with their love. The message was one of mercy, of feminine tenderness and forgiveness.

The group then began a new song. After listening for some time, I asked Junior what it was.

"It's the presentational dance," he said.

"For who?"

And then I heard a woman call out my name.

Priscilla, Junior's wife, was dancing out from the group in my direction, her arms cradling a sealskin vest. I kept looking around, and Junior just laughed. Priscilla brought me up front and put the vest on me. Delores's family was "adopting" me, a symbolic gesture of belonging to the clan.

It turned out that the sisters and Delores had been making the vest for weeks, always scrambling to hide it when I came over. The week before when Delores had turned her back on me in the kitchen, it was because the sisters had come up behind me with measuring tapes, secretly mapping my shoulders and torso for the vest. She had turned away not, as I thought, because she was mad at me, but to keep from laughing.

The vest had two large ravens on the back that stood over a fountain of silver beads that flowed from a hole in the earth. Delores said that the silver beads were waves spouting through the blowhole at Mountain Point, and also represented me going out into the business world. She said the two ravens on either side were her family and her watching over me.

They gave me a Tlingit name, *Gányaa*, their word for *wood-packer* or *beaver*, symbolizing a hard worker. They then had me dance with all the clan people clapping and hooting. Junior was next to me, showing me how to dip and swing my shoulders in a crouched stance like a raven.

Each Tlingit has three parts of their lineage: the side or moiety, then the clan, and last the house they belong to. I was now *Raven*, in the *Beaver* clan and the *Halibut* house. As I danced, I thought of Old Man, his ageless eight-ball eyes looking at me. The Buddha of the deep was now my brother, my Halibut house kin. Two hundred feet below the surface, he held a piece of my soul, a piece about survival and persever-ance and deep wisdom for me in the dark. I was glad that he was down there.

Chapter 32

ESCAPE FROM
HOOVERVILLE

Summer into Fall 1988

I was *outside*, as they say in Alaska, at my mom's apartment in Bellevue, Washington, finishing up a quick business trip for Cape Fox Tours. The phone rang. It was Crow.

"Hi," she said, her voice slightly tentative.

"Hey, what's up?"

"I'm in Seattle," she said.

I had trouble making sense of it. "What the heck . . . ," I said. "What are you doing here?"

There was a long pause. "I'm at the airport and heading back to Ketchikan."

"Um, I thought you were in K-Town."

There was another long pause. "I . . . I had an abortion," she said.

Time stood still. It felt like a train had run through my head—a derailment, followed by a bewildered silence.

"What," I muttered. "I didn't even know . . . you were pregnant. What . . . ?"

She spoke quickly. "I didn't want to tell you, I didn't want you to get mad, I knew you wouldn't want it."

"Mad . . . ? I'm, uh, I'm—I'm upset you didn't tell me." There was more silence on her side and a sniffle. "Don't go back tonight," I said. "I've got a plane tomorrow. I'll come and get you." Anxiety swept through me, and I had trouble finding my keys and left the apartment three times, each time turning back for something I forgot.

She was there on the sidewalk, outside baggage claim at SeaTac, with only a small carry-on, crying. On the ride back to my mom's, she told me she went to a clinic on Capitol Hill and that the staff had been amazing.

"Listen . . . I'll, uh, I'll pay the expenses."

"No," she said. "It was my decision. You shouldn't have to be involved."

I insisted on paying just the same. Crow and the two girls were just eking by; she was on financial aid from the state.

The next day, we flew back to Ketchikan together.

In Hooverville, I walked into a strange enchantment. The trailer home was warm and clean. While I was down south, Crow had come in and painted the entire place. It looked like Alice in Wonderland, high on Mad Hatter tea. The walls and ceiling had been sponge-dabbed into an impressionistic mural of Chagall-like figures liberated from gravity flying about from floor to ceiling. It began in the back on the bedroom ceiling and ran down the walls and even over a chest of drawers.

A young girl flying a kite arched across the bedroom of a powder-blue, yellow, and white sky. The kite string and clouds led down the hallway and into the living room where the kite sailed with a flock of swans above a landscape of trees and a lake.

This incredible, surreal, and playful artwork freed Hooverville from its sordid gloom, infusing it with a renewed feeling of happiness and lightness. Crow was an astonishing artist. But as I walked from room to room, a slight unease settled in. Everything was neat and tidy and warm, but almost too neat. It seemed my things had been gone through, drawer contents rearranged, and in the closet, a box of journals with the lid partly off. An unexplainable heaviness came over my heart. I should have run up and told Crow how amazing what she had done was—the art was astonishing. But I wasn't sure how to feel about it. Was it a marvelous gift or an invasion of privacy?

But Woody had gone up to Crow's, and so, reluctantly, I trekked up the hill, not sure how to respond. Carrie and Rachel were playing in the forest front yard. They had built a series of connected dens with cardboard boxes and blankets thrown over as cover. Inside, they had set up a table with Raggedy Ann dolls, plastic dinosaurs, a Barbie, and a stuffed owl and orca. They had made mud cakes for dessert. Their new mutt, Springer, followed me in, making all of us unwelcome to the tea party.

"No boys or dogs allowed!" Rachel declared, and we were thrown out.

Woodsmoke was coming from Crow's stack, but no sign of her. I tossed the Frisbee down the hill a few times for Woody, who expertly snatched it between trees before it hit the ground. Springer ran after him like a madcap fool, but never seemed to pick up the intent of the game.

Carrie and Rachel came out of their den.

"Tea party over?" I asked.

"Owl and Orca want some cookies," Rachel said. "They don't like our mud cakes too well." They headed into the house. It was warm and resonant with the smells of sweet potatoes and apple pie baking. I walked into the kitchen.

Crow was there, passed out on the floor, as if she had dropped in her tracks. I bent down to shake her. She responded as if she were slowly waking up.

"Oh," she said woozily. "Wow!" She leaned on me and found her way to a chair.

"What happened?" I asked.

"I must have passed out. I don't remember. I was heading to the oven, and that's the last thing I remember." She told me then that she had a rare blood disorder and that sometimes she got so overwhelmingly tired that she would pass out. Yes, she assured me, she was getting treatment for it.

I stayed long enough to make sure she was recovered and went back down to Hooverville. It all was feeling *curiouser and curiouser.* Woody got an omelet for dinner to make up for my three days in Seattle.

Weeks passed and sleep was ragged, only a few hours a night, partly because of the growing strangeness around Crow and Hooverville—but also because of the pervasive stress of the work in Saxman. Every day, worries arose about how the day would go. Would the crew be there to meet the tour buses? Would the dancers be there and on time? Who wouldn't be speaking with me today?

After a fitful night and hearing that four busloads of tourists were on their way to the village, I went in early and hung around my favorite place in Saxman, the carving shed, where master carver Nathan Jackson toiled. The carving shed was my shelter from the storm, where Nathan held court. In the shed we had built for the tour, Nathan designed and created large totem poles, wood-panel clan crests, masks, canoes, and carved doors that he sold to museums and collectors around the world. He was the most dependable part of the tour.

Nathan was a solid, strong man of medium height, with a handsome, high-cheeked face. He was Sockeye clan on the

Raven side up near Haines, where he learned commercial fishing from his uncle. One day, while disk-sanding the bottom of a seiner, a mixture of dried jellyfish and copper paint powder got into his lungs. He started coughing up blood and ended up in the hospital for two months. To pass the time, he began carving miniature totem poles, a practice that stayed with him and turned into an obsession that became a lifework.

Nathan embodied raven trickster spirit. He danced at gatherings with a large, carved raven mask and moved with such fluid energy and spontaneous humor, you felt you were seeing a five-foot-eight-inch bird. He liked to have a laugh and usually had the last one.

"You know," he said to me, with a friendly, innocent air as he slowly wandered over, "my wife made up a pot of cedar tea last night."

"Yeah?" I said. "How was that? Didn't know you could make cedar tea."

"Oh yeah," he said seriously, picking up a chip of cedar bark from the ground. "You take this and peel it *real* thin, and then drop it into a pot and boil it . . . about twenty minutes."

With Nathan, I had learned to wait awhile after he said something in case he was trying to sucker me in. I just stood there with the piece of cedar in my hand and looked at him. He could usually keep a straight face for about ten seconds, and then he would explode in laughter. The Tlingits were great practical jokers, and Nathan was the best of them. He couldn't hold it in, and his face blossomed with a laugh that contorted his body.

"Do you put sugar in it?" I asked.

He looked at the piece of cedar in my hand and belly-laughed again.

The buses arrived, and some tourists entered the shed. Nathan went back to work on the thirty-foot pole he was making for a museum in DC. Little did the visitors know that the short man in coveralls working and whistling in this simple wood building was one of the country's most prominent master carvers. He had the skill to bring out the designs and animal spirits already inside the tree. He was working away on a salmon figure on the pole with his adze when one of the tourists wondered if he could ask a question.

"Go ahead," said Nathan slowly in a put-on serious, basso profundo voice.

"Do you use traditional paint on the carvings?" asked the man.

A pole historically was painted red, black, and aquamarine, from natural substances. Nathan stopped working and was thoughtful. "Yes," he said, slowly and gravely. The tourists from Phoenix, Minneapolis, and Sarasota waited. You could feel the weight of anticipation in the air.

"Yes," he said again, playing the noble, reticent Native American. "I use traditional . . ." Then he paused, considering.

The tourists waited. The other carvers stopped working.

"Dutch Boy!" he yelled. Nathan laughed and laughed, looking at me with a grin that could span mountaintops. His eyes gleamed, and as the tourists laughed, he yelled, "Dutch Boy!" again.

Being with Nathan was a daily respite from a job that was taking a huge toll on me. Despite the success of the tourism business and the employment it was bringing into the village, more and more of the Saxman folks met my efforts with suspicion. As things began to succeed, they figured someone was getting the best of them. They were feeling the stresses too. It was hard to preserve an authentic presentation of heritage deluged by buses pulling in every day. There is a line where performance becomes perfunctory. Folks were working hard, but being on the clock day to day didn't suit them. Some of the villagers were beginning to take their frustrations out on me. The day before, one of the elders, Estelle, who thought we had underpaid her hours, exploded in anger as I was showing her how we had figured her paycheck.

A few months later, David Goodenough came to town, and I met him for dinner at a diner along the water to talk over my troubles. It was magic hour, an early fall evening in Southeast Alaska, the sunlight so clear you could taste it. A trawler, its outriggers spread, rolled up the Narrows, circled by yellow-illumined seagulls.

I told him I had no idea if what I was doing in Saxman was right. "What if this is all my thing," I said. "Here comes another white guy . . . I mean, Dave Sisewell thought he was doing right."

"Dave Sisewell's projects failed. Yours didn't." He took a sip of his tea. "One never knows." He smiled. "Sometimes the smallest interaction may have a lasting impact on another. You have no idea, twenty years from now, how it affected the kids who learned the dances and songs during this time. You'll never know what influence it's all had on the teenagers you hired, or the elders, for that matter, or the community having a carving center, a store, a tribal house."

"Then how do you know to keep going?"

"You do what you feel is right, what feels right in your heart and conscience, and you move forward, trusting in that. That's all you get to know."

"Yeah . . . but I'm running on empty. I feel if I don't get out of Saxman, I won't make it. And yet it's all still too dependent on me."

"I agree. You do need to leave," he said. "And you are also right: you can't leave yet." He continued, "But you can make a commitment, internally, that you *will* leave. Put a date on it, say a year from now. That way, you give the universe a better chance to conspire with you for it to happen. You don't need to tell anyone, but you have to make an internal commitment

that you are going to leave. If you just wait first for the circumstances to be right to leave, that day will never come."

The *Western Titan*, a blue-and-yellow tugboat, toughed
on by, bound for Wrangell towing a barge of freight. I was
drinking a lot of wine and felt my face flushing, suddenly self-
conscious, knowing David knew of my dad's history.

"Can I say one other thing?" David asked. I nodded. Smiling
in his reassuring way, he said matter-of-factly, "You need to get
away from that woman." He had met Crow once on a business
trip when the three of us had lunch together.

"What?" I said, a bit taken aback by this sudden shift in
the conversation. Things were definitely strange with her, but
I wasn't sure about abandoning ship. "Why do you say that?"

"Why are you trying to rescue her?" he replied.

"Rescue her? I don't know that I'm trying to rescue her. But
she does need some help, yeah. She's got two kids, and . . . I
guess I can tell you this. She had to have an abortion a short
while back. I can't really leave her in the middle of that," I said
convincingly, at least to myself.

"Do you have any evidence that she actually had that
abortion?"

I was flummoxed. "What? Of course, she did. What do you
mean? I picked her up in Seattle at the airport."

"Did you see any paperwork, invoices from the clinic,
post-treatment instructions, pain medications, anything like
that?"

"Well, no," I replied.

He took a large breath. "I want to suggest to you that she
never had one."

"What are you talking about?" My head started to reel.

David breathed slowly. "I suggest you are involved with
someone with their own world of made-up facts."

At first, confusion arose, then slowly a bunch of things
began to rotate into place. A sense of doubt that I had never

voiced. The visit where she was passed out on her kitchen floor? It was a strange sight. It didn't seem real at the time, something wrong with it. She had been laid out too perfectly, on her side, her legs arranged, her body positioned exactly in the middle of the floor. Not the way someone would look if she fell. Stranger yet, Carrie and Rachel had just stood there, too, not saying a word, looking down at their mother, like they knew we all had to play along.

And then in Seattle, she had been crying at the airport but seemed robust and healthy, not like someone who had just undergone a medical procedure and needed some downtime. She never referred to any paperwork from the place or took any medications or talked on the phone with the clinic. I was swirling.

On the drive back to Hooverville, a deep anger began to simmer, fueled by the glasses of wine. After pulling into my driveway, I was teetering between reality and unreality, belief and disbelief. I walked up to Crow's place, where Carrie and Rachel were on the living room floor coloring. Crow was in her bed, looking at a *National Geographic*. Bizarrely, it was an issue devoted to the nine months of a baby in the womb. She showed me a photo of a fetus about four months along.

"This is what our baby would have looked like," she said.

I was seriously creeped out.

"Crow, can I ask you something? You know that clinic you told me about, on Capitol Hill?"

"Um, yeah, what about it?" She kept on looking at the fetus pictures.

"So, what was it called?" I couldn't get over the feeling of prying, opening up something best left alone.

"I can't remember," she said. "It was up there in the hospital district, near Madison somewhere."

"Oh, and the doctor's name, remember him?"

"Umm, no. But he looked a bit like Woody Allen. Why would I want to remember it?" she said, narrowing her eyes.

My heart was racing. "I'm just wondering, that's all. Did you get any paperwork from them? You must have."

"Yeah, yeah, it's around somewhere. In a drawer, I think."

I really wanted to believe her, but had to press on. "I'd like to see it. Can you get it now?"

"Now? I'm in bed! I'll look for it later. I really don't know where it is."

And then like a ray of sun that faintly burst through months of Alaskan cloud cover, I knew Goodenough was right. I stood looking at her, almost afraid to speak.

"It didn't happen, Crow. Did it? It wasn't real." My voice started to shake. I wasn't comfortable with getting angry. My dad taught me to keep it stuffed in. So like a hunting dog kept on a leash all its life, my anger swelled and turned to frustration. I wanted to punch a wall.

She acted shocked. If she would show me anything from the clinic, I would fall on my knees and beg forgiveness. But she said she didn't feel well enough and, anyway, she might have burned it.

"It wasn't something I like to be reminded of," she said.

I walked out without saying another word and roamed the roads with Woody. When we passed the devil dog, I looked at him with such pure vehemence that he just stared back passively, without running at his chain.

Back in Hooverville, I was completely spooked. Her entire life as she had told it was full of holes. What about the neighbor who was stalking her or her abusive husband, or having a child via a surrogate father? Was any of it real?

There was a knock on the door. It was Crow. I got up and opened it.

"Hey," she said in a carefully crafted way. "Can we—"

"Go away!" I shouted, and slammed the door on her. She stood there on my porch in silence for maybe three minutes, like a specter, and then left. My heart was beating hard.

With little sleep all night, as a murky dawn crept into the mobile home, I realized I had lost my way. The time had come to get out of Hooverville, away from Crow. It was time to get more remote and back to the adventure of solitude.

Chapter 33

SHAKRI-LA

November 1988

Swirls from my paddle strokes unwound behind us in the emerald sea. Woody sat in the back of our new craft, the *dogyak*, a green, eighteen-foot canoe-kayak with a semi-open cockpit. The dogyak was on its inaugural run, sixteen miles from town, north of Knudson Cove Marina in Clover Passage. The rough, steep coastline was combed with evergreens that exposed an occasional cabin. I envied the inhabitants this far out of town, their nearest neighbors animals.

Spooked by us, a heron in a tree lifted and squawked like a pterodactyl across the blue morning. A couple of river otters swam by, not paying us much mind. The dogyak smoothed through the water like a hand along a silk kimono. I wasn't much of a meditator, but the rhythm of kayaking brought me into a state of mind as wordless as the ocean itself. My shoulders ached a bit from the repetition of paddling, but I liked the slow burn it gave my midriff rotating from one side to the other, plying our way up the coast, with Woody behind, a silent, serene mariner, taking in the world as it was.

We rounded a point and swept into a half-moon bay below hills of cedar, alder, and hemlock. There, just beyond the dog-yak's contoured bow, I beheld a vision right out of a dream. The surprise of it made me miss the top of the water with my paddle, lurching me slightly forward. We drifted silently toward the center of the bay where an unpainted gray house on stilts stood alone.

It looked like a wizard's hut.

I was breathless. What was this place? There seemed to be a rough path up the barnacled beach where stones had been cleared away, and we aimed at it. I learned later, this cleared underwater path through the rocks had been a haul-out for Tlingit canoes whose inhabitants came to this bay for berries and salmon.

We crushed against the sand. It was then I became aware of a gentle *swiishhhhh* through the woods. Unseen on the other side of the hut, a waterfall gentled through the air. I stepped out, pulled the craft up the beach, and made my way along the rocks toward the wizard's den. Woody followed, tail high and eyes brimming. Two massive trees, a three-hundred-year-old cedar on one side and a Sitka spruce on the other, framed the house. Along its base, wild sea asparagus grew. The roof was steep and covered in faded cedar shingles. A large picture window looked out to the bay. Inside could be seen a couch, a lamp, and a telescope. Upstairs, a small square window opened to a loft.

A raven made sounds like the anchor of an old chain dragged along the ocean bottom. Around the side of the house toward the woods was a small work shed covered in mosses and ferns. Through the trees, I now could see the sinuous body of the waterfall that tumbled out of the forest, white as an angel, splashing across black rocks into the bowl of a green lagoon.

I turned back to the house. Two alder trees stood as gateway guardians before a short set of stairs that led up to a porch. Through a door with small glass panes was a mudroom with rain jackets and rubber boots strewn about. I knocked. No one came, but compelled to step forward into this mystery, I tried the knob and found myself in a kitchen nook with a rough, round table looking out to sea.

"Hello!" I yelled. No answer.

I proceeded into the living room feeling like I had snuck into a movie theater without paying. The house was perched high off the beach, the dogyak resting on the beach below. The sun glinted a golden path to the edge of the shore. Across the bay, two remote, tree-filled islands held down the horizon. A distant skiff softly pursed the coppery sea.

I then said out loud, surprising myself, "I have to live here." The words tumbled from my mouth as naturally as leaves dropping from a tree. And then, unbidden, a name rose up inside me. The name of this place: Shakri-La.

For a week, I asked around town about the hut sixteen miles north. Someone told me they thought it was Steve Reeve's place. I couldn't believe it. There were 14,500 people in Ketchikan. Steve Reeve was the lands planner at Cape Fox who had helped me develop the tour program and was now resurrecting the hotel project. I dropped everything and tore out to Saxman.

"Steve," I said, busting into his office. "Is that your place north of town, the house by the waterfall?"

Steve sat back. "Funny you should ask," he replied. "The people who have been living there for the past eight years are thinking of leaving."

Destiny is a word suggesting "from the stars." And sometimes it comes right through the door for you.

Chapter 34

BETWEEN TWO WATERS

July 1989

Inside Shakri-La, Woody and I sat on the *sea couch* looking out over an undulating carpet of aqueous blue ink. The tide was high and the shore subsumed. The sea had come up beneath Shakri-La, making it appear as if we were perched on the bridge of a starship looking over a liquid galaxy, nothing but water below us. An occasional salmon kissed the underside of the mirror, broadcasting soft ripples that rolled into stillness. It seemed the entire surface of the ocean breathed as one.

Behind us, through the window on the forest side, the *swoosh* of the waterfall filtered through the trees. For six months now, I had slept between these two waters, the bay on one side, the waterfall on the other. Between them, a new animal was emerging into the world, a human animal no longer answering an insidious call to be successful or loved on someone else's terms. A hidden animal who had come to Alaska to unravel his upbringing and escape a time-bound, corrupted culture that had trained him as one of its servants.

I reveled in being alone and in the forest again like the Taoist mountain hermits of China. They grew tea and dwelled apart from the chaotic world of man. Unlike ordinary people, they were not anxious. It seemed their wisdom was achieved by living alone among the elements. These felt like my kin.

> *Men cannot see their reflection in running*
> *water, but only in still water.*
> *Only that which is itself still can still the seeker*
> *of stillness.*
> *The mind of the sage, being in repose, becomes*
> *the mirror of the universe.*
>
> —*Chuang Tzu*

Shakri-La was more expansive than the Little Red Cabin. It stood like a cedar clan house on stilts above the beach, the center point of the bay. Its wood-framed living room was simple with a woodstove in the back corner. Through an open doorway, a breakfast nook overlooked the beach. On the second floor, a small office hid among the branches of a spruce. I slept in a roof loft with a small window that opened to the sea. Sitting in the pink tub offered a cedar-framed view of the bay. Down a steep set of stairs from the kitchen, you found the basement, with a three-thousand-gallon water tank filled from a hose that ran to the top of the waterfall.

Shakri-La had been barged here in the 1940s and pushed as high up the beach as they could get it. But they hadn't accounted for the extreme tides. With a nineteen- or twenty-foot tide and winds behind it, the basement filled with seawater—rocks, sand, and seaweed sloshing through.

Shakri-La was an enchanted box with soft, nature-washed walls. Here with Woody, my life could expand into a deeper level of solitude. At Shakri-La, I felt truly, for the first time, the possibility of home.

A bad back had been ailing me for weeks, injured in an almost surreal way. The previous year, David Goodenough had coaxed an internal commitment out of me to leave Saxman. But as the deadline had grown closer, it seemed unrealistic. The Native tourist enterprise was still dependent on me. It had never been my intent to have it be so, always figuring I'd leave it once it could stand on its own legs. But on the very first day past my internal deadline for leaving, stepping out of The Palace in the Cape Fox lot, a disc herniated in my lower back—just getting out of the truck.

My body had fulfilled its contract. I had made it a promise to leave, and it was not going to let me break my vow—even if it had to bust my back for me to get the message. As the healing took its time, I felt beyond burned-out and trapped in Saxman with the walls caving in. I called Goodenough, who listened patiently as always.

"Here's what I want you to do," he said after hearing my travails. "Hang up the phone and ask yourself, 'What do I need to do for myself right now?' Just that. Do that and listen to the answer." With nothing to lose, I agreed and hung up.

At that moment, like a moving target in a carnival shooting gallery, a Princess cruise ship appeared along the horizon. It was steaming in from Sitka, on its way to disgorge its passengers in Ketchikan, many of whom would travel to Saxman. A familiar wave of anxiety flared in my belly. What would go wrong today?

My eyes closed. *What do I need to do for myself right now?* The answer was immediate. *Sit here and watch the sea.* It was as if a deeper part of me spoke. As soon as I heard the words, a sense of spaciousness opened around me, a sense of relief. Before the answer could be rejected, I called my assistant, Claudia, at Cape Fox Tours and told her I wasn't coming into work that day.

By unplugging the phone, the sea became my TV. Treating my back with the utmost care, I only took trips for food and to the bathroom. All that mattered was the mesmerizing play of currents, northern pintails paddling by, salmon surfacing, and seals popping up their dark heads to look around. All the while, Woody lounged and went in and out the door, delighting in our newfound paradise, our waterfall oasis in the world.

Every day now began with the practice: *What do I need to do for myself right now?* This unassuming exercise, asking it to myself and then listening to the honest answer, changed my life. It empowered me in a clear and profound way to *seek first the kingdom within.* That week, I only went to work a day and a half out of five.

Sitting on the sea couch was also unveiling an insight, shedding light on something obvious. I had walked into Saxman naively—attracted by the culture and a desire to make a difference. But Saxman was also a place where alcoholism was strongly prevalent. Nearly every home in Saxman had been touched by it in some way. In denial of my own trauma as a child of alcoholism, I had unknowingly sought out a place where its shadow was always near.

"Why do I get in these messes?" I asked David. "With Crow, with Saxman?"

"Because you are a rescuer," he replied.

I bristled. "Isn't it okay to try and help people?" I asked.

"Helping is fine, if it's asked for. But you step in when it's *not* asked for. And then you get personally hooked." He took a deep breath. "You do it to take their pain. It's pretty common behavior for a child who has emotionally neglectful parents.

The child reaches out to help, but the problem is, the child is like a bare wire. You weren't insulated. You never experienced healthy boundaries."

I had never heard that word before. *Boundaries.* Tears formed behind my eyes. Reaching out for the father, *to take his pain . . .*

"You take their pain into you. And you get attached. It's your unconscious way of seeking belonging and family," David gently kept on. "It feels noble to you. You step in to help. It seems as if you are blowing fresh air into their lungs, showing them a way, a new life. Trouble is, a lot of victims, while appearing to want to change, are afraid to leave their situation. They often don't want to take responsibility; they do not want to be rescued." He paused. "It's a form of abuse actually."

"How so?"

"Fools rush in where angels fear to tread. You infiltrate people's lives and start to move the furniture around as if they asked you to. That's what you did with Crow. It's what you did in Saxman. Trouble is, they most likely didn't really want to change. Eventually the victim will turn on the rescuer and will make the rescuer their imagined persecutor."

This is exactly what had happened with Crow. I had stepped into her life as a quiet protector of her and the girls, and she had accepted my help while portraying herself with imagined threats on all sides. These illusory threats further fed my desire to protect, employing the caretaker role and the sense of family it gave me. But as involvement with her deepened, I also sought love and validation from her. The stories built up, the drama increased, skeletons began coming out of the closet. Since leaving her, she had gone around town with tales of how I had abused and abandoned her. I had become her latest imagined persecutor.

A similar dynamic was about to unfold at Cape Fox.

Chapter 35

WHIPPING POST

September 1989

The board received my transition plan to exit Saxman at a weekend meeting. My goal had always been to create a Native-owned business built around cultural practices and not dependent on me. Cape Fox Tours could stand on its own now.

The plan included my official resignation and three months for me to stay on as a consultant to help hire and train my replacement. This came as no surprise to the board. I had been talking about it for a while, but had made a large mistake. I hadn't stopped by Delores's to tell her about it personally, preferring to avoid it, as she would likely get upset with me.

Three of her children sat on the board. They looked over the proposal, and then the vice chair, Robert Strong, asked the chairman for a recess. He and the other two members of the Strong family ushered me, along with Ben David and Craig Burger, into Burger's office. The silence in the air was as thick as seal grease.

A hint of something coming occurred the week before, but I wasn't able to piece it together at the time. The village had held a potlatch to raise a new Nathan Jackson pole, a replacement of the boy with his hand stuck in the oyster shell, a story I had long identified with. During the potlatch, my adopted Tlingit uncle, Junior DeWitt, announced my name and publicly thanked me for what I had done. It felt strange; he had never done anything like it before, the way his voice was, like he was sending me a message that he was on my side.

"Close the door," Robert told Ben solemnly. The calm before the storm. Positioning himself behind Burger's desk, Robert turned to me and suddenly jabbed his finger across the desk at my face and exploded. "You used us!" he shouted. His face turned red. "You used us!" he screamed again.

As his anger boiled over, I should have known better but sat down and got very quiet. That's what a kid does around an alcoholic when things explode and escalate fast. The dad erupts, spitting venom, and you get really still in hopes you don't get bit. The more Robert's ire stormed over me, the more outwardly calm I got, which seemed to enrage him further.

"You used us!" he shouted for the third time, his face twisted in rage. He pointed to my proposal. "You get paid, but what about us?" he shouted on. "What about the elders who made all of this possible? What about the dance group?"

Delia, Delores's oldest daughter, stood next to me. She was a woman with an honorable bearing who had been an ally, always supporting me, telling me many times to keep going even when a lot of people seemed opposed. She had been a vocal advocate in the challenge of taking tribal traditions into a commercial realm.

And she, like her older brother who was screaming at me, was also a recovering alcoholic. Delia's face was darkened over, radiating vitriol toward me. Willie, the youngest who often called me his "little brother," stood against the wall, looking down.

"Willie?" I said, implying, *You know this isn't true. Brother?* But Willie looked down and stayed silent. He could not speak up against his older siblings.

I felt utterly alone. Because of my work, the dance group was making money. More members of the Strong family had jobs in the village than any other family. Totem poles were being carved and raised in the park. There was a tribal house, a village store, and Saxman teenagers were having the opportunity to work their first jobs.

The greatest sound in the room besides Robert shouting at me was the deafening silence of no one speaking up for me. And I hadn't yet learned the bigger lesson . . . to stand up for myself. I tried to speak but got too tangled up inside. I stood up and slipped off the beaver skin vest the family had made for me and dropped it in the middle of the floor.

"You shamed this," I said through tears and walked out.

I fetched Woody from downstairs, piled into the truck, and roared off down the highway. Behind the wheel, my tears turned to steam as a potent anger filled the cab. In a moment of serendipity, just as we left Saxman, someone on KRBD put on the Allman Brothers' "The Whipping Post," a hard-driving, angst-riddled blues jam. I turned it up real loud. I was done with Saxman, done with the formal working world, done with fractured families and relationships. Woody was the only family I needed and a trustworthy one at that.

Over the next few days, my emotions swung wildly between hurt and rage. Sometimes I would go back into the scene and see myself stand up and shout back at Robert. Other times, I walked around the desk and embraced him in a hug as he cried. There was, despite it all, an affection that had developed between that family and me.

But it had been naive of me to think their symbolic "adopting" me came with true belonging and trust. I wasn't really part of their family. Like an immature, well-meaning puppy, I had wandered into a village with a high rate of alcoholism that had experienced little or no social change in a couple of generations and had begun to move things around. My work put a larger public face on Saxman, and with cultural support and financial help from Cape Fox and the backing of Delores, the City of Saxman, and others, it was succeeding economically and culturally.

Most of the Saxman people had joined in support once they saw it was working. But the Strongs also felt it was reliant on me, and if I left and it failed, the dishonor would fall to them. They got afraid. The hidden distrust of me as a white person rose from beneath the surface. They thought I had led them to the edge of a cliff and was abandoning them.

The part of me that was searching for true family and belonging in the world had imagined a deeper connection, but it had been a mirage. I had been "performing for the prize," and, yes, rescuing, when it had not been asked for. A kind of conditional love had developed between the Strongs and me; but I wasn't family, not really. The deeper truth was, I could leave the village, and they, by and large, couldn't. I was a white guy, a faux-Indian, not really a member of the clan.

Now the "victim" had turned on the "rescuer," and the rescuer felt like a victim. As Goodenough had told me, my own unseen savior complex had gotten me into this soup. What happened was inevitable.

For the next three months, out of a deep responsibility to the enterprise succeeding, I did keep coming to work on contract. But I always looked away when passing Delores's house. Eventually, my replacement got hired, and though things were shaky for a long while, the cultural tourism program ultimately persevered. Not for a long time would I step foot in Saxman again. The wound cut too deep.

Chapter 36

MORNING GUN THERAPY

February 1990

My feet stood steady inside the black high-top Chuck Taylors, feeling the crush of sand. The day was cold and quietly opening its eye—the sea smooth as a glass plate, the waterfall frozen with but a trickle into the lagoon.

Six large booms shook the sky. They came from the blue-black cylinder of the .357 magnum in my hand as I stood with nothing on but skivvies and shoes, a leather holster slung around my waist. The gun was pointed at a dead-stand tree at the edge of the beach. The blasts echoed over the water, bounced off Clover Island, and sailed back across the crystal sea.

Woody was intently watching from his perch inside on the sea couch. As burnt-oil gun smoke wafted into my nostrils and my ears began to ring, the anxiety and rage inside me calmed, as if a demon had been exorcised.

This was *morning gun therapy.*

Its origins could be traced to some treatment for my lower-back pain, which had become chronic. A friend referred me to Jacqueline Bagwell, a naturopathic doctor in Seattle, who greeted me at her office with an elfin smile. She gave you the sense she knew a few secrets. She seemed able to discern causes and recommend treatments through a sophisticated mixture of science and mysticism.

She looked at me, glancing past my head as if she saw invisible things around me. I was telling her about the stresses of Saxman, about leaving and settling into Shakri-La, and about the deep pain in my back that continued to plague me.

She peered at me, listening closely, saying, "Uhh-hmmm," as if trying to unravel a mystery. She tilted her head to one side and then unexpectedly leaned forward in her chair and placed her hand smack in the center of my chest.

"What's happening here, Ward?"

I felt the pressure of her hand on my chest but felt nothing underneath. "I don't know," I answered. It was a strange sensation, almost as if she had a hand on someone else's body.

Leaning farther forward in her chair, she asked again, "How does it feel in your heart?" She turned to the side, as if she could feel inside of me.

"I feel numb," I said.

Jacqueline leaned back. "A lot of rage," she said quietly as if she were slightly in awe of its depth. "A lot of anger inside you, Ward."

I had no idea what she was talking about. I felt nothing and certainly didn't feel angry right then.

"What will you do with that anger, Ward? The pain in your back originates from here." She tapped me in the chest. "If you don't do something about it, it will manifest down the line most likely as some kind of heart condition." She fixed me with her clear blue eyes. "In the meantime, it's keeping you out of meaningful love relationships, too."

This hit home. Though I occasionally had girlfriends, I always left them in my intense drive for solitude. But the truer reason, perhaps, was the fear to let anyone get too close.

"You can't think your way out of anger, Ward," Jacqueline said. "You can't reason your way out of it. You've got to get it out physically."

"How?"

She led me over to a couch and instructed me to punch on a pillow. It felt stupid, but I gave it a try and punched and punched. I felt nothing, but she encouraged me to keep it up for a few more minutes. After some time, breathing heavily, a cold ache rose in my chest. Something in me had awakened.

In the months after, almost as if Jacqueline had given my body permission, the deep ache in my chest came to be felt as anger. Following doctor's orders, instead of sitting on the couch and wondering about it, or drinking coffee, which made things worse, I would get up, yell, stomp my feet, or hit a pillow, expecting that would do the trick. But without fail, the anger would return. I began to wake up in the morning with a fire in my chest.

The anger felt locked in cellular memory, an anger stored up before I could even talk. The more it surfaced, the deeper it went. Anger from the womb, anger from rejection of the mother—anger at being overpowered by the father. Anger at Saxman, anger with the way the earth was being treated. Anger at myself for losing years inside a three-piece suit. Anger at God. Layer after layer of it surfaced. I went from being a man who didn't even know he was angry to a maniac stomping, screaming, or hitting things, and I couldn't really explain it to anyone. Jacqueline was right: thinking it away did not work. Only physical actions got it out of my body.

One day, as the anger burned a small campfire in my chest, I impulsively ran upstairs, reached into the closet for my .357, strapped it on, went out to the beach, and fired six quick rounds into the dead snag. I felt clear and cleansed.

And so morning gun therapy became a ritual, once or so a week. I'm not sure Woody ever got used to it, nor did the ravens, herons, river otters, or distant neighbors, but slowly, over time, this and other physical means of expressing my anger nudged aside an armoring around my heart.

After six months, Dr. Bagwell's anger management had taken root. Mornings felt relatively anger-free, and creative inspiration was flowing into writing and photography. Miraculously, I also had a new girlfriend, a massage therapist from Portland. Alyssa was intuitive, fun, and as kind as they come. We had only been involved a few weeks when she decided to come to Alaska. Shakri-La was a wonderland to her. In a ride in the dogyak one day, immersed in the exquisite beauty of this land, she said, "Being with you is like being on an acid trip."

But it wasn't me: it was Shakri-La and the stunning enchantment of Alaska in spring. That night, we turned down the couch into a bed so we could wake to a view of the ocean. I slept fitfully, though, unused to having other than a dog sleeping next to me. In the morning, opening my eyes in the dim dawn, my old nemesis, anger, sat on my chest. It felt like a hot poker in my thoracic spine, and nothing ostensibly had caused it.

Alyssa was sound asleep, as was Woody, who had joined us on the bed sometime during the night. I lay there awhile, hoping the anger would subside, but it stayed like an undersea volcano in the bay of my heart. It felt ancient, tectonic, a life of its own.

"Damn!" I whispered. I had to get it out of my system. Upstairs I went, belted on the .357, and came back down. On my way through the living room, Alyssa woke up. On her first morning in Alaska, she saw a naked guy coming toward her with a gun strapped around his waist.

Fire rose into my throat. I kept walking through the room and just managed to say to her, "I can explain later." I pulled on my tennis shoes, ran down to the beach in front of Shakri-La, and . . . *Blam! Blam! Blam! Blam! Blam! Blam!* Six shots boomed over the water and bounced off the house. The echoes faded, displaced by a distinct ringing in my ears. Cold air brushed my back, chest, and legs, and with the sun just cracking through the bowl of the day, I emptied the six hot shells into my hand, my anger released into the morning air.

Holstering the gun, I went back inside, where two sets of eyes as big as half-dollars met me. Sitting on the bed, sixteen miles out of town, in a remote cabin, was a terrified young woman, holding a blanket up to her chest, looking at someone she didn't know well with a gun belt around him. Next to her was a dog, confused by the primal call of gunplay he was not able to answer.

Alyssa returned to Seattle and, with her, our short-lived relationship. But things were not at an end. Five weeks later, she called.

"I have to tell you something," she began. I could feel myself numbing on the spot. That potent and provocative pause on the line. The gerbils in my mind were running in every direction.

"I'm pregnant," she said with bare excitement.

Surf scoters bobbed on the sea, the sky was cold and silver gray. I exhaled a long breath. This was not how I saw my life unfolding—with an unwanted child. Someday, I intended to be a father, but I saw it as part of a long-term union. The relationship with Alyssa didn't feel sustainable to me. She could tell I didn't share her enthusiasm about the baby, and it surprised her. What more happiness and purpose could there be, a woman in the bloom of pregnancy? I played along as best I could and, after hanging up, lay on the sea couch trying to get behind the reality of being a dad.

Woody had taken off again, too—something he was doing more and more often lately. He seemed to not like Shakri-La as much as our other places. The beach here was rocky, not like the sandy world at the Little Red Cabin or the more social environment at Hooverville, where he could go adventuring or visit neighbors. Shakri-La was located at the bottom of a long hill, cut off from the world of people and other dogs.

How could this work out? Maybe just let Alyssa raise the kid? But I felt the guilt of that, how the kid would always be looking out for its dad, with me somewhere in the world, not answering the call. I felt bewildered and alone, about to become a reluctant parent. It was not lost on me, an unwanted child myself, that I was passing that experience on to my own child-to-be.

The next day, Alyssa called, crying. She had had a miscarriage.

There is a dynamic tension that holds nature seamlessly together, how decay leads to new growth, how one creature eats another, how the tide tugs against the earth. And how relief and grief flooded through me at the same time. In the face of the immaculate and abundant seascape out my window, I wept and felt free again and even more alone.

Chapter 37

WINNING THE LOTTERY

April 1990

Besides wrestling with occasional bouts of loneliness, one drawback to my withdrawal from the formal work world was the slow bleeding of my savings. Ventures into photography, theater directing, and, of course, radio were keeping me afloat, but only on a week-to-week basis. This was the necessary wasteland on the economic border one had to cross between commerce and art.

To be an artist was completely outside the widest frame of reference in my family. Even to consider an artistic livelihood was foreign, not something deserving to be taken seriously. To be in our family was to be responsible, rational, and to work inside a company or organization, rising through the system. You didn't question the box. An artist wasn't the profession of a real man. Not like accounting.

Accounting was safe to me, a structure and refuge from an emotionally unstable upbringing. Though accounting was the dire opposite of my nature, it had made me feel secure buttoned up in a three-piece suit in a world of rational rules and boundaries, where emotions were contained and not expressed. To see the numbers on the page add up and all fit together in a linear and defined whole was comforting and satisfying. It gave the illusion that I was on firm ground.

Unstable economic ground was shifting below me now. My financial "security" involved calculating how much money there was and the number of days it would last. Typically, my on-hand funds would stretch two to three weeks into the future. Many times, on my last crumbs, the phone would ring and an art job would come through: teaching pinhole photography in the schools, or directing a local play. But now with debts piling up, the system was breaking down.

I called my dad.

Douglas Edward Serrill had retired after working forty-five years for Boeing. He helped design the B-17 bomber in World War II, the Saturn V rocket in the '60s, and the 747 in the 1980s. But the aerospace business was a heart-attack machine. It chewed its career workers up and beat them down until they surrendered to the few years they had left. It worked out a bit differently for my dad, though. A year into his retirement, he won the Washington State Lottery—three million dollars. Diligently, consistently, for two years, every week, he had bought ten dollars' worth of tickets at the same convenience store. One of those tickets paid off mightily.

"How bad is it?" he asked, when I told him about my financial woes. His voice was tight. Immediately I wished I hadn't called.

"A few months to steady things out," I replied tentatively. "To get me on my feet."

"How much?"

My heart was thumping. I wanted to hang up. "Um, maybe six, seven, thousand?"

The response was silence. The silences always made me anxious; never knowing what came next, I grew very still.

Dad was a man raised in a cause-and-effect world. You did right, did the responsible thing, worked hard, and you got rewarded. You weren't given things. You screwed up, you got punished. There was no gray area.

"Don't you think it's time to go back to accounting?" he asked rhetorically, making the answer clear. He wanted me to stop living what he saw as a crazy, erratic life. Like most parents, he just wanted me to be happy, but in his rational, mechanistic worldview, to attempt to live as an artist was foolish. It made absolutely no sense to him.

I looked out at the desolate sea. How could I even begin to explain?

"No," I said. "No, I can't go back to that. I just need some help with this transition. I just need some help right now."

The line was thick with tension. "Why don't you put together a plan," he said finally, "and send that down to me."

After hanging up, anger began to inflame my chest. I walked upstairs, got the .357, went out to the beach, and fired off some rounds.

A few weeks later, my dad and his new wife were on their way up to Ketchikan. He had remarried after running away from the detox hospital and divorcing my mom. His new wife was a fellow social drinker he had been having an affair with for some time. Dad had felt trapped in a marriage that had died, trapped in a job that had been slowly killing him, trapped inside a family that he had sacrificed his life for. And he wrapped it all inside a blanket of guilt he could not shed nor express. He never mentioned the hospital, his escape, or the divorce to any of us kids. But he did stop drinking, going dry the last seventeen years of his life.

For the trip, he had outfitted his twenty-five-foot Sabrecraft into a long-distance traveler, with a fifty-five-gallon drum on the back for extra gas. The day after they arrived, we were having dinner at their hotel. One of the reasons for getting together was to talk over the business plan he had asked me to put together. It forced me to reason out a few things about my future. The business plan involved paying off my debts, and enough for six months of breathing room to develop a photography and video business in Ketchikan. Though my original estimate to him on the phone was $7,000, the revised plan called for a more sustainable request, a $12,000 loan.

We had a nice dinner at first. Since Dad had won the Washington State Lottery, he hadn't changed much, but the windfall had relieved him of a lot of stress. He now lived in a nice condo, drove a big-muscled Firebird, was about to buy a bigger boat, and wore nicer clothes. While waiting for dessert, I presented him my plan. He read it over slowly, then put it aside and didn't say a word. Dessert came and his silence persisted.

"What's up?" I asked. He just shook his head. As a kid, these silences often led to his eventual eruption in anger. His wife and I talked clumsily, and she glanced up at him to encourage him to join in, but Dad stayed as quiet as a dammed-up river. He paid the check and we all went back to their hotel without a word.

He and my stepmom disappeared into the back bedroom while I sat on the couch listening to their hushed argument, not sure if I should go or stay. The tension in the room was almost unbearable. Had I asked for too much? Maybe it was best to leave now. I was great at leaving, and the thought of being with Woody at Shakri-La felt good and safe right then.

The bedroom door opened. My dad came in. He threw my proposal on the couch.

"Well, you've really done it this time, haven't you?" he muttered with a quiet menace.

I was baffled. Three decades of frustration rose through my body as through fissures in the dark earth. I exploded off the couch, hands ripping at the air.

"What? What!" I screamed. "What did I do?"

He had never been screamed at by anyone in his entire adult life. It was not something you did in this family. He had never shouted at his alcoholic dad, nor had his dad before him. Authority ruled, plain and simple. *Emotions were to be submerged.* He walked away from me, his back a huge and impassive wall.

As a kid, my name for my dad was "Big Bear." In dreams, I was often running from bears. Sometimes, they were trying to get into the house; other times, a bear's face would be right next to mine. If I moved, I would die.

"I just don't . . . ," I began, tongue-tied. I followed him into the dining area where he stood next to the table. He brimmed with indignity. Dad was not to be challenged in any way.

"My whole life," I blurted out, "I've always been so *afraid* of you!" Having finally said the unthinkable, I felt vulnerable and embarrassed.

He stared down at the table, one hand on the back of a chair. The silence was again impenetrable. I wanted to run.

"I guess, I've just been a terrible father, haven't I?" he said with finely honed, guilt-laden skill.

My heart was a fire truck speeding down a small street with the siren on. I dropped my head and started to cry. I cried the tears of Wassy, who had never been held, and the tears of the adult son who knew it was hopeless to try and be understood by his father, the tears of years struggling unsuccessfully to win his love. It was hopeless. A fire had burned down all the exits.

And then I heard a sound I never expected.

Choked with a soft and thin voice, my dad said one word: "Don't . . ."

He stepped over and clumsily wrapped his arms around me. He held me. For the first time in my life, he held me.

My tears rolled down Big Bear's back.

"Don't cry," he said and wouldn't let me go.

A few years later, my dad died at seventy-nine of a bad heart. But not before a call one night to Shakri-La, on ship-to-shore radio, from the *Ecola*, his thirty-two-foot cruiser. After talking briefly, there was a hesitation on the line.

Then, with a voice high and lean, he said, filled with a rare passion, heard by every boat listening within fifty miles, "I want to tell you . . . I want to tell you that I love you very much!"

I don't remember another word from that call.

Chapter 38

FREEWOODSIN'

April 1990

Ketchikan's one main road snakes thirty-three miles from end to end and is branded with seven different names: South Tongass, Stedman Street, Mill Street, Front Street, Water Street, Tongass Avenue, and North Tongass Highway. Poked and smashed out of rock hillsides, it winds its way past bars and churches, small stores, industrial warehouses, logging outfitters, marine suppliers, Quonset huts, gravel pits, sheds, shops, busted machinery, homes, bait shops, and canneries, all the while clinging for its life along a craggy, thrashing sea.

Woody was riding shotgun along North Tongass Highway, leaning forward into the windshield as he did when he sensed we were aiming for the woods. The April day was brisk, daylight now returning to our northern world. Throughout the fall and winter, at best six to seven hours of muted daylight eked out from beneath a mass of clouds as thick as attic insulation. All fourteen thousand of us on the rocky island were beginning to wake up from a long, collective sleep and, like bears, blinking our eyes into a newfound spring.

The gravel road terminated in a cul-de-sac shaped like the bulb of an onion against the backdrop of raw forest. We parked near a yellow *End* sign with its ever-changing calligraphy of bullet holes. Woody trundled out of the truck and plunged into the woods, gone in a flash, leaving me to follow and fight through a twist of wine-red blueberry bushes erupting with spring leaves.

Woody was playing his part in an adventure called *free-woodsin'*, a central ritual of our relative life of solitude. It was simple: park the truck alongside the woods, get out, and let Woody lead. *Freewoodsin'* was not about following man-made trails but discovering untrodden paths to see where they went.

My rubber boots sank into the muskeg, the squishy green-brown blanket that lies over much of Southeast Alaska's land-scape. Muskeg is pocked full of secret black ponds around which spring all manner of bog flower, berry bush, sphagnum moss, and stunted, twisted trees with an occasional dead snag mixed in. A vehicle left overnight on the muskeg would be half swallowed by the next morning.

Lunch Creek, a wild and sinuous waterway, clambered down from the mountains to our left. If we got lost, we could always follow it to the sea and make our way back to the truck. Water-heavy tangles of berry vines and hemlock branches brushed me on all sides. A hundred feet into the woods, my clothes were already soaked. Breaking free of the web of under-brush, I followed Woody down animal trails that led over mossy logs, through mud holes and mountain-washed creeks.

Woody was gone, though, long gone. He had raced sure-footed into the woods, exploring the resplendent bouquet of wild creatures and earth tones. I hustled instead a bit west, then north, to play hide-and-seek with him, a game in which he was so far undefeated, as he was able to follow my trail a week after it had gone cold, even in a downpour.

I ran zigzag, slogging over a ridge, and hid behind a giant red cedar, pushing my body up against it. The tree's downy skin was deceptively yielding and fragile, yet I felt its strong protection for the heartwood beneath. Maybe trees were the inspiration for the term *thick-skinned*. It didn't mean one was unfeeling or insensitive; rather, it meant anchored in one's own being, protected and yet available for those who earn the trust to go beneath the surface. Four feet around, the cedar rose high and straight into a gray-blue sky. With slow, deep tree breaths, and my hands around the trunk, I reveled in the feeling of being outside of time, no one knowing where we were. Here in the woods, my mind free, with a sense of wild beginnings and secret, supportive roots beneath my thirty-three years of life.

Suddenly bursting out of the bushes, slopping full speed across the clearing, loped Woody, his eyes ablaze with joy. He had followed his nose right to me and arrived long-tongued, thrilled and panting. He snuffed around some skunk cabbage and then disappeared again into the woods, following the feral incense of deer, mink, wolf, and a hundred others.

On toward one small clearing to the next, with little or no trail to follow, my hands were as important as my feet, pulling myself along frilled cedar boughs and scratchy spruce. Up and over hills and down through creeks, stumbling into sinkholes, finding my rhythm in a rubber-booted dance through a water-logged obstacle course. The sour flower-smell of skunk cabbage permeated the air, and dragonflies zipped about. A kingfisher barreled by on a mission, and a raven called.

I went up a hill and over to a meadow, and there, in the middle of a big, oozing black mud hole, was a vanilla-colored dog, up to his face in muck, happily waiting for me. He rose like the creature from the black lagoon—now a chocolate

Lab—then wheeled away, disappearing again, slopping mud in his footpads.

Deeper into the forest, just before a stream crossing, I came across a giant cedar root wad, its downed trunk stretching hundreds of feet through the woods. It was a nurse tree with a half dozen young saplings rising from it. An opening in the root wad looked like a television with its screen knocked out. Here's what was showing on the Woods Network today: A winter wren hopped from a branch; a single sun streak illuminated a path through the sword ferns; a big-leaf maple frond fell, and all to a creek performing original music. No commercials and all the drama I needed.

We scrambled five more miles upstream until we met Lunch Creek and followed the shoreline to a small clearing by the bank where a trio of enormous spruce trees pressed into the sky. A small, terraced waterfall cascaded into a wide, deep pool, tempting me to jump into the pristine cedar-tinged water. Woody hopped along the bank, wanting me to throw something in, but he eventually left me alone to mind my own business.

The raw loveliness of this place, akin to a sacred temple, stunned me. This hallowed ground seemed to have been created with a single purpose in mind: to express an inexplicable divine beauty, a beauty so potent that silence was the only reasonable response. Being here made me suddenly feel closer to God. How could such exquisiteness as this be ignored in the world? And how could anyone cut down such temples, just to make a buck?

A varied thrush shrilled to the poetics of the creek song tumbling into froth. I lay back on the sandy rise, the press of the ground warm as the spruce giants enveloped me with their mossy arms. Sunbeams sifted through limbs and tapped the water's surface into golden sparks.

Woody was in his own world playing. He was immersed in a game he invented: *stick overboard!* He found a stick and carried it to a high spot on the bank where he lay down. He dropped it from his jaws, and his tail wagged. He stared at the stick resting on the edge of the bank, completely sure it was about to throw itself into the water.

He nudged the stick with his nose, and then watched intently. Another nudge. The stick edged closer to the bank. Another tail wag. Then a miracle! All by itself, the stick fell into the river! As if it were the most surprising thing he had ever seen, Woody jumped up, raced a few feet downstream, and sprawled through the air, flying into the pool with a tremendous splash. He swam after the stick as if his life depended on it, saving it just before it disappeared around the bend.

He swam back with it clenched softly in his mouth, snorting, then crawled out on the bank, dropped the stick, shook off, picked it up again, and finally raced up to the high point, where the game began all over again. He played *stick overboard* for at least a half hour, completely immersed, never once noting me.

Being Easter weekend, a baptism was in order. I stripped down and walked barefoot over the cool, elastic earth, then took a run and a headfirst flying leap over Woody into the pool. A torrent of icy water poured around me. Whooping and hollering, I began to swim downstream and collided with a big dog nose. Woody had crashed in after me, and his underwater claws were scraping my chest raw. I had to leap upstream into deeper water to get away from him, but like a sea otter after its mama, Woody kept coming. The only choice was to turn him around and swim together toward the riverbank, his dog face right next to mine.

We climbed out, my testicles the size of grapes. He spun his body around to shake me afresh with ice water. *Hoo-hoo!* I yelled. Woody ran up and down the bank, assuming now we could both play *stick overboard.* I stood naked in the sand, watching my chest breathe and the tiny dots of water shine over my body. The droplets plopped to the ground. Drying in the sun, an inexhaustible happiness filled me.

I looked down to see a bear print in the mud next to my foot. A single print twice the size of mine. A black bear, who came to the river presumably for a drink or for salmon. I pressed my hand into the bear's prints and ran my fingers across its deep claw marks in the sand. Looking over my shoulder to the forest, five miles from the road, I felt suddenly watched and vulnerable.

Mosquitoes quickly ganged up and drew me out of my reverie, prompting me to scramble into my clothes and bid farewell to Lunch Creek. Keeping the creek to our right as we hiked out, about a mile from the road, we encountered an older tourist couple hiking in. They wore newly bought rain slickers.

The man stopped and asked with a hint of boredom, "Anything up there?" He pointed behind to the forest where we had just emerged. My head reeled. *Anything up there?*

"Nah," I replied. "Nothin'. Just a bunch of trees."

He shrugged, and the couple turned around. Maybe they were looking for a souvenir stand or something.

Woody and I beat it, *freewoodsin'* back to the truck.

Chapter 39

DOG SAMADHI

June 1990

In Shakri-La bay, the water temperature near the surface was tolerable, if not delightful—though down a few feet, an aching cold lurked. I floated naked, in the late-afternoon sun, wearing an orange life jacket, with a second one under the ankles. The underwater world *chittered, fizzed,* and *pinged* in my ears while tiny air bubbles from clams and mussels rose and tickled my back. Water droplets beaded on my chest, while the mind imagined warm lips kissing them away . . .

In the sky, a bald eagle crossed, slow and great-winged. I closed my eyes, and my breath slowed and deepened, falling away from the world, feeling like a sea god floating in dynamic calm—

A huge sucking sound erupted near my ear, and water splashed over my face. *"YaaaaaaaWWWWWWah!"* I yelled in alarm, and a shot of panic blasted through me. Something had grabbed me, and I struggled to get my feet on the bottom.

My head rolled back to see Woody's excited eyes. He had a corner of the life preserver in his mouth and was turning us 180 degrees to tow me headfirst toward shore. Rescued by a clown dog! His big breath gulps were like the guffaws of a practical joker who knew he had pulled off a great gag.

Woody had a thing about the color orange. He always snapped into attention around an orange object. With a Frisbee, ball, or life preserver, he knew if he concentrated on it long enough, it would eventually move and he would retrieve it. He ferried me to the beach and deposited me helpless, laughing, my head bumping into the sand. He crawled out of the water and shook, showering me all over.

We had lived now at Shakri-La for nearly a year and a half. Layers of fatigue from working in Saxman and the formal work world had melted away, and my life had grown quieter. Solitude was a battery charger for me, day to day, moment to moment, renewing my energies. My only social life was Saturday forays into town to host *Over the Edge*. The other five or six days a week involved little contact with other humans. My phone lay unplugged most of the time.

It felt like living inside a continuous and timeless poem. When alone, one has the opportunity to take in the natural world in a deeper way, uninterrupted by words or by another, standing silent before creation, stunned by its beauty over and over again.

I was never truly alone, though. Living aside a waterfall, time evaporated and animals drew near. From the water came salmon, seal, sea lions, orcas, river otters, and ducks. From the air: herons, eagles, ravens, cranes, winter wrens, hummingbirds, bats, owls, thrushes, and a dozen other songbirds. The woods brought coyotes, squirrels, mink, wolf, black bear, and deer.

Friends were beginning to call me "Ward Serrill, man of solitude." More than ever, I was determined to mine the gold that solitude held. The biggest bugaboo working against my plan, of course, was my longing for a woman. But a passion for solitude and a woman do not often go hand in hand. As my friend Buell wrote from Seattle:

> *You are fishing for mermaids in the shape of*
> *God...*
> *You have perfect conditions and life without*
> *female headache.*

Shakri-La existed in an intertidal zone, as was I between what I had been and what I was becoming. The tide flowed by me and through me, soothing pains of the past, while the sound of the waterfall eased itself inside my blood and fell away to the sea.

Sitting on the sea couch one day, about a hundred yards out, I spied something crossing the bay amid the glittering and ruffled waters. My binoculars revealed a large cedar tree, about sixty feet long. It must have broken free from one of Louisiana-Pacific's log booms. I watched for a while with a growing sense of dismay. That was two cords of prime firewood floating by out there, but the idea of making the effort to corral it right then deflated me.

It was time to meditate, a daily practice for me now. Meditating was slowly revealing that the vast majority of my suffering was rooted in thinking—my thinking that something was somehow wrong in this moment or in me or in my circumstances. The more time, though, immersed in nature, the more my thoughts and opinions settled. The daily work involved becoming engrossed in simple awareness. It became apparent to me that nature existed in a continuous state of becoming, where the ten thousand things (including me) arose and fell of their own accord, in harmony with a greater whole.

The afternoon sky bloomed oyster-shell pink. Woody jumped up next to me. He, of course, had no opinions about any of this. He just looked through the calm eyes of the Tao always. At that moment, a heron at the far side of Shakri-La bay stretched its Tai Chi body and pushed off from the point. It flew slow and low over the calm water toward us. It reached the shoreline but kept coming until it opened its entire six-foot wingspan right before us, and then settled on the roof directly above. A protector spirit to oversee our meditations, perhaps.

My eyes closed, and the sun poured orange warmth behind the eyelids. The quiet swoosh of the waterfall and the smell of incense filled the air. Time passed, and I fell into a state of profound quietude. Perhaps an hour went by, maybe longer. Only peripherally aware of my body, behind my eyes, the light grew brighter, suspending me in a state of near breathlessness.

Sometime later, my eyes then opened to the deepest, richest sunset, full of brazen pinks, lemon yellows, and burnt orange. The seascape radiated inexplicable peace, not even a duck or seal or salmon interrupted its grace. A note from Buell pinned up on a card below the window read: *When you are in the Absolute Present, God shines through that transparency.*

Meanwhile, I had forgotten all about Woody, but there he was still next to me, sitting up looking out at the same sea, his eyes focused softly inward, undisturbed and unmoving. Was Woody meditating? Perhaps he was immersed in a state of oneness that saints and mystics called samadhi. Was Woody floating in *dog samadhi,* a borderless frontier of pure being? Perhaps I was sitting next to a master soul.

The cedar log had drifted halfway across the horizon. Woody awoke from his rapture, got off the couch, lay his head over my leg, looked me in the eyes, and wagged his tail slowly and deliberately. He knew if he stared at an object long enough, it would eventually move.

So that twilight, we invented *kayak logging*. It only took fifteen minutes of paddling to reach the enormous cedar. I pulled out a rusty iron spike and pounded it into the end of the log with a hammer, tied a rope to it, fastened the line to the stern, and began to head home. But paddling a kayak while towing two tons of tree slowed down our progress a bit. By the time we made it to Shakri-La an hour later, Woody was asleep in the back.

The tide was still medium high. I roped the cedar to the large spruce tree next to the house. As the tide receded, it beached the cedar, and over the next three days, I cut and split the prize for our winter wood. All this physical activity made me feel vibrantly alive. Hardly a thought entered my mind the entire time. This must be similar to Woody's joy. He was a creature that roamed about the earth seemingly without thinking. He existed in an elemental state of being, with a keen awareness of the land under his paws.

He knew where to be.

Chapter 40

WOODY MEETS
DARK BROTHER

July 1990

The dogyak was outfitted with a few snacks, a Big Dad Beef Stick for Woody, and some drinking water. Clover Island, about a mile across the bay, was the goal. Anticipating the adventure, Woody carried the orange life preserver down to the boat, jumped in, and made his way to the back.

With a sweeping paddle, we were off across the aqueous universe. It was a high, bright day with a layer of thin clouds as if filtered photographic light illuminated the sky. The only sounds were the bump of the kayak paddle and the squawks of a few flying ducks with squeaky wings. I looked back to see how Woody was doing. He was sitting on his haunches like an intrepid seafarer, while behind him, Shakri-La seemed a toy house with a line of silver-gray woodsmoke curling above its roof.

We smoothed across the blue-green sea until reaching the small bay at the south end of Clover and floated awhile before pulling around to the back side of the island where a steep forested wall rose from the sea. Hugging close to it, we found a hidden grotto behind some low-hanging cedar limbs just big enough for the dogyak to slip into. The slosh of the water echoed between tree and rock. Underwater, veiled by the cedar branches, orange and purple starfish clung to the rock wall, and lime-green anemones retracted their sticky, squidgy tentacles from my touch.

Timeless time passed, and I reveled once again in the knowledge that no one knew where we were. There was an exquisite feeling of freedom in that. After some floating meditation, we pushed off and headed down the channel. Woody began moving around in back, tipping the boat. We had worked on this problem a lot, and he knew he had to sit still when we were in the dogyak. A seventy-five-pound passenger thrashing around at the wrong time could end badly. *Siéntate!* I called to him. When he moved again, I yelled louder, then stopped paddling and turned around. Woody was standing up, looking intently over the back end. *Siéntate!* I said more forcefully. Slowly, ever so slowly, he lowered his rump, but never for a second broke his concentration on the water behind.

What held his attention? Ten feet behind us, a black dog head with two enormous eyes emerged from the deep. Woody's dark seal brother stared back at him, intent and silent. When the seal slipped out of sight, Woody waited, every cell of his body electrified. A moment later, the water dog resurfaced, now only four feet behind. He locked eyes with Woody and flared his large nostrils. He had long white whiskers around his snout and two small earholes on the sides of his smooth head.

Woody lifted his nose slightly and sniffed three times, reading the air for any clue about his strange new companion. I felt a kinship with seals, but as far as the seal was concerned, there was only one creature in the boat, and that was Woody, as big a mystery to the seal as he was to Woody.

As the seal floated closer, Woody strained forward, trying to get as near as he could without standing up. The pinniped's large, dark, impenetrable eyes looked at him one last time, then as silently as he had arrived, slipped back into the watery underworld.

Woody stared at the water for some time before slowly turning his head to look at me. His eyes were full of wonder and question. Woody had met his doppelganger, his other self, his shadow, his seal brother.

As we paddled home, twilight now taking over the sky, I wondered about my own shadow, a loneliness that lurked just below the waterline. Would it emerge someday, as did the seal, and look me directly in the eyes, not to be denied? The path of solitude eventually turns inward, and involves sometimes long and lonesome work. I understand why most people talk about getting free but ultimately turn away from the quest and stay in their conditioned lives and self-imposed jail cells. Freedom requires, at last, a journey to explore the pain that lurks beneath the surface. When you stop running, it begins to arise.

Buell wrote:

> *Ward: An odyssey into the underworld, descending to meet his own wound.*
>
> *To heal the wound is to become the hero of his own life.*
>
> *He seeks mate but will not find as he does not trust giving up. At birth, mother abandoned son and to fully commit to another has become too vulnerable, fearful, considering the wound*

inflicted. His odyssey then is to heal that: which is ironically to abandon all fears.

It is no doubt best for you to give your heart away freely and always and most of all under every condition, because what you give away is what you have . . . to be free, in spite of the apparent odds.

Chapter 41

LAST DANCE WITH DELORES

July 1990

One day, someone from Saxman told me that Delores was in the hospital. It had been nearly a year since I had seen her.

Dread coursed through me as I stepped out of the truck in the hospital lot, imagining the icy welcome of the Strongs. Maybe they'd even ask me to leave. Delores could be so domineering and abrupt when she got stirred up. But this *was* my Indian mother. She had adopted me into her clan—and, with her, it had felt more than symbolic. She had gone along with my ideas on the group singing and dancing more regularly. She had supported the efforts to build the tribal house, the carving center, and the village store. She had welcomed me into her house whenever I had stopped by. She named me White Raven and taught me how to say a few words in Tlingit. Despite all that, she had to have been the one behind the family's insurrection against me, or at least supported it.

Here it was, my greatest fear: rejection from the mother.

My mom, June, had tried to commit suicide when I was four months from being born. She told me she had felt distressed and depressed at having her fourth child at age forty. She took sleeping pills and was out for days. After my birth, she was unable to touch me, nor express physical love. This base cellular rejection has influenced my entire life and relationships and made me hypersensitive to any dismissal from a feminine figure, especially a surrogate mother.

A lot of research speaks to the plethora of neural connections that are formed by touch and bonding with the mother in the first thirty minutes after birth. For me, it wasn't just thirty minutes; it was forever. No skin-to-skin touch, breastfeeding, or physical expressions of love. It's taken decades to pioneer the emotional circuitry from my heart to my brain— literally the capacity to be able to feel and express emotions. It's not something you can really explain to anyone, except to therapists. But you will perpetually feel that there is something wrong with you, and your family and siblings especially will never understand.

The hospital elevator rose slowly until it pinged at the second floor. Down the scrubbed hallway, past gurneys, wheelchairs, and the nurses' station, the place smelled of pine cleanser and Clorox and resounded with the squeaks of rubber soles against the polished floor.

I came to Room 261. The first bed was empty, but in the second one near the window, Delores lay looking out at the gray skies. Hanging from a stand next to her bed was an IV bag, and she was hooked up to a heart monitor. Another machine beeped quietly. She was completely alone. *Maybe I should leave?*

She turned her head. As soon as her eyes fell on me, she burst into tears. I went over to her side of the bed, where she lay in crisp white sheets with an oxygen tube in her nostrils. Her skin was pale gray, like that of an old sea lion. Her eyes were opaque and wet with tears. I held her hand and gave her some water from a straw.

Her eyes cleared, and she whispered as she squeezed my hand weakly, "My White Raven. My little White Raven . . ." We held hands and my tears joined hers. We stayed that way for a while, no one else came in the entire time. We hardly spoke, and then she slept.

The next day, I heard that Delores, my Indian mother, had died that same night in her sleep. She was now, like me, suspended between two waters. Hers the ocean of life and spirit, mine the waterfall and the sea.

Chapter 42

THE WATERFALL

August 1990

On a dead-end street, I pulled up to the house and walked up the porch. No need to knock when it's among friends. A fellow DJ from KRBD, Carolyn Minor, lived there. She hosted a folk music show and played a sweet guitar. There it was against the wall, a Martin D-28 that had played a starring role in one of the most unlikely guitar rescues of all time.

Carolyn and her husband used to live on Pennock, a three-mile-long island across from Ketchikan, accessible only by boat, with no roads. They lived in a cabin near the beach. A few years back, a bunch of us had gone over for a party and whooped it up late into the night, with a bonfire to keep us warm from the cold. The next morning, Carolyn discovered two things. First, the laundry they had laid out in the creek to wash and forgot about had frozen under the ice. Her laughter turned to dread, however, when she realized she also had left her $1,500 Martin out on the beach in its case. The tide had been unusually high that night, and it had carried her darling out to sea. We went to search for it in kayaks and skiffs, but it was hopeless. Carolyn went into mourning.

Days later, however, a coastguardsman found a guitar floating in its case in the Narrows. It was a Martin D-28, dry and unharmed. It had survived days at sea, in and out of tides and brushes with sea lions, storms, rain, and wind.

Some things are destined to return home.

Woody was a free-roaming dog and was taking off a bit more frequently these days. Most of the time, he came back to Shakri-La on his own, announcing his return with a signature single paw scratch at the door. But more and more, I had to go retrieve him. There he was, as usual, on the carpet, boxing and gnashing teeth with his best friend, Bob, a rascal of a black dog, about three-quarters Woody's size. Woody had been gone from Shakri-La for a day, but it hadn't caused me too much worry, nor had I bothered calling about him. It had become so commonplace for him to come over to Carolyn's to visit Bob that she had started to consider Woody family.

It troubled me when he took off, but his regular trek to Carolyn's felt like a safer venture than most. It was two miles up the highway, but along a pretty lonely stretch. I had seen him traveling there once, in the ditch cruising along, staying well off the road. That Carolyn lived down a small dead-end street made me a bit more comfortable. Ultimately, I put my trust in the universe. I knew we were destined to be together until the end, him on the porch, an old dog living out his days with me.

Back at Shakri-La, the water tank in the basement had run low. It was time to fill up, which meant a trip up the waterfall. We began the hike to the top of the falls, a two-horse gas pump in hand. Woody wagged his approval of the adventure, as being anywhere outside, with any excuse, anytime, was the meaning of life. It was a clear and bright day, a perfect time to fill the tank. If too soon after a rain, the water took on an orange cast from the runoff of soil and seepings of cedar root, devil's club, and blueberry.

Just as we hit the woods, we came across a river otter ambling overland three feet in front of us. His sea-wet fur was the same color as the soil. It was all Woody could do to not tear from my grip and go investigate this latest wonder of the world. We watched as the otter disappeared over a ridge, and then Woody took off, tail wagging wildly, combing the woods for a clue to this strange being's nature.

We hiked back and forth across steep ridges and bumped our way softly through the woods until we encountered a major obstacle—an enormous cedar tree that had fallen six months past. Its root wad was twenty feet in circumference uphill. The entire tree, too large for my chain saw, had fallen down a steep incline and was difficult to maneuver around. With one hand, I climbed up the six-foot trunk, holding the pump in the other. Woody raced easily uphill, around the root wad, and cut across to rejoin me on the other side.

Before going on, we detoured for a ritual adventure. The path to the falls was straight ahead, but off to the left, across a ridge, ran a precarious trail. I set the pump down and made my way along the rocky ledge, holding on to blueberry branches to keep from plummeting forty feet to the rocks below. Woody dutifully followed along, knowing not to try and squeeze by me in such dangerous terrain. I pulled myself sideways for about thirty feet before stepping around the final bushes to a ruder, more primitive path. From here, we descended steeply a few ridges to a landing called the Tree Mitt.

The Tree Mitt was a hemlock—or a family of them— composed of five trunks that rose from a common base. The trunks stretched horizontal toward the sea before turning upward and forming what looked like a large baseball mitt.

With a sheer drop below, I lay back in it as if caught in center field by Willie Mays. The Tree Mitt resided on a hidden shelf midway up the falls where the water slopped and dropped across black-slicked algae-green rocks. Maidenhair ferns swayed back and forth from the wind of the waterfall as if making hand mudras with the cedar branches. A single water drop dangled from the end of a fern before falling, replaced by another and another. The entire roaring falls was powered by a multitude of such single drops from far up in the forest and funneled down countless seepings. Patient water, one drop at a time. Like our lives, each of us is formed one moment at a time, drops in some great river of existence, flowing out to sea.

The Hindu mystic Ramana Maharshi talked about what he called the sruti note, a Sanskrit word meaning "that which is heard." It is the note that underlies all other notes. The falls of Woody Creek sounded the sruti note of this landscape. Its continuous music, framed by alders, hemlock, and cedar, set the tone for my time at Shakri-La, reaching out, a pair of hands that coolly massaged my spine. The falls filtering through the forest also filtered through me, stilling my blood and thoughts.

But it was time to get back to work, so I crawled out of the Mitt, traversed across the treacherous ledge, recovered the pump, and continued the ascent. At the top of the hill, we scrambled down a small cleft in the bank to the creek above the falls and jumped over to a little island of rocks and sand in the middle. Seaward, five feet away, the waterfall rolled over the edge in a silky, seductive flow. One false step, and I'd be salmon meal in the lagoon below.

Brown clumps of foam—trapped air bubbles and organic compounds from the forest—floated out to the sea, toward the distant green outline of Betton Island. Each fall, salmon returned to the lagoon below. They were remnants perhaps of an ancient race of their ancestors, now following some primeval song to where the land was once not so lifted up and they could leap its heights and travel to the creek's upper pools. Woody and I had tried often to find its origin, a mysterious place in the mountains, but we were always beaten back, exhausted and lost in the steep, rough terrain.

I turned and hopped upstream from rock to rock around a few bends of the creek to a surreal sight: an old, rusted car frame half submerged, water rushing through the shell of its busted windows and doors. How had it gotten here? Probably some drunken fools had shoved it over the bridge a bunch of years ago. It had rolled, pushed by the power of thirteen feet of sometimes thundering rain, to be lodged firmly in the streambed. Logs and debris had built up around it.

I climbed through the driver's door and sat on an old stump in front of the steering wheel, looking out the empty windshield, my arm around my girlfriend, driving down the creek. An ouzel danced crazy knee bends on a river rock and dipped his beak into the water. Woody was on a small island of sand, snapping at dragonflies.

Snaking down through the forest ran a quarter mile of three-quarter-inch black hose. I hooked up the pump and gave the starter three quick pulls until it putted to life. Soon, fresh, clear, woods-rich rainwater was pulling down the hill to fill the tank in the basement of Shakri-La.

Chapter 43

THE NIGHT THE SKY
FELL INTO THE SEA

August 1990

By twilight, the three-thousand-gallon tank in the basement was full. As night descended, the cedar crackling in the wood-stove warmed our haven. Woody wanted a breather, and I went out on the porch with him. The Milky Way appeared dim at first, then became clearer as my eyes adjusted. As a shooting star burned through Cassiopeia, the Milky Way twisted through black holes, supernovas, and constellations, a wondrous, heavenly cup of flowing waters.

Down on the beach, as Woody's silhouette moved against the star-reflected sea, sparks of light erupted in his paw prints in the wet sand. Phosphorescence! I rushed over and tossed a rock into the bay. Green glittering fireworks exploded in the dark water. Woody waded in and stood, knee-deep, looking down at air bubbles rising up his forelegs like tiny glowing balloons.

Perhaps the Tlingits, who used this place long ago as a seasonal camp, witnessed this watery phenomenon on some enchanted nights. After gathering goose tongue, sea asparagus, and wild peas from the beach; huckleberries and blueberries from the forest; and salmon from the lagoon, did they sit in wonder before these same mysterious lights as their children threw stones into the sea?

I rushed to the side of the house and grabbed the dogyak. Woody jumped in, and we paddled away fast, leaving behind spinning galaxies with each stroke. And then, as if the miracles would never cease, the northern lights appeared in the sky, neon green and shimmering. I felt Woody's calm presence behind me as the swift quietness carried us along. Rivulets of water fanned out from the bow like luminous jade pearls strung along a black necklace. Everything in the night was lit and on the rise and suffused with beauty.

My hands in the cold Alaskan water appeared to glow like eerie Halloween props, dismembered and green tinged. Bubbles rose from the seafloor like the iridescent thoughts of crabs, the musings of blue mussels, or perhaps stirrings from an underworld sea lion den. Darkened forms of kelp waved, circling, like harem girls.

The northern lights ebbed and flowed across the heavens, veiling the stars behind. The illuminations intensified and pulsed until a central green ring appeared directly above with ribs that spread down and widened to the top of the islands across from us, as if we were under the dome of a cosmic yurt. My yelps and hoots echoed through the night.

I then paddled toward the source of my life's melody, the waterfall. The companion chorus of my sleep, of my dreams, of my longings. We pulled toward its siren song pouring into the lagoon. Suddenly, shapes below us burst to life. Three sea otters, like underwater *Fantasia* characters, flipped and twisted in space, leaving sparkling trails behind. Woody leaned over the side to watch them.

Phosphorescence is caused by an algae bloom of millions of dancing dynoflagellates and the waterfall seemed the source of this rave as it stirred up a vast, luminous pot of lime-white incantation from the head of the lagoon. The light appeared to emanate from a glowing underwater cave. The dogyak nosed into the falls and the sea around us surged with radiant light. I yelped again and paddled to hold fast against the star streams that flowed past us, splashing my head and face with glimmering water.

As the waterfall shoved us gently out to sea, more underwater streaks appeared at the head of the lagoon. Miraculously, the humpies had arrived to spawn! They came from thousands of miles away to congregate beneath the falls on this very night. Like underwater shamans, they flashed and flexed, leaving lustrous trails behind them.

As we floated in the stillness, the Milky Way reflected across the water as if the sky had fallen into the sea. I knew then with a deep sense of rightness that the upcoming winter would be pregnant and rich and magic and everything would, as always, work out.

Woody, of course, had other ideas.

Sirius was rising in the east.

Chapter 44

PAW PRINTS IN
THE SNOW

January 1991

The air was cold, the clouds high and gray. Soft snowfall blanketed everything. My boots squeaked and breath misted as my lungs strained climbing the trail from Shakri-La. At the top of the drive, just before the highway, a single line of heart-shaped dog paws was pressed into the snow, as elegant as calligraphy, leading away from home. My heart ached.

Three days before, it had started to snow on my birthday. I was thirty-three, Woody was seven, halfway through his journey. We had celebrated by going cross-country skiing. We started along the snow-covered highway, Woody loping alongside my skis, his feet padding in the new snow. We reached a small road leading into the hills and pushed up it until finding a path through the forest that roughly followed Woody Creek.

The sun lit the white-covered trees, my eyes aching from the glare. A couple of orange-breasted robins watched from an alder limb. The trail was pocked by the footprints of rabbits, mice, and mink. Woody grabbed mouthfuls of snow on the go or stopped to dig his snout underneath, ferreting around for the hideaways of furry creatures. The going was strenuous, at least for me. Along a clearing at the top of a ridge, we stopped and looked down on Woody Creek as it crinkled through the soft woods toward Shakri-La.

We started our downhill slide, Woody running just in front of me, looking back with joy in his eyes. The cold wind brushed my face, and a pleasure, perhaps equal to his, filled me.

At the top of the pathway to Shakri-La, I unhooked my skis and started walking down the steep hill. It began snowing again. Woody jumped off the trail to search the woods. At the bottom, he didn't follow me inside; he would come along in his own time.

I stoked up the woodstove, unplugged the phone, and kicked back on the couch.

With a couple of cords of firewood dried, ready, and stacked; the kitchen full of food; and the water tank brimmed, I felt rich and settled in for a lovely retreat, nothing but the simple bliss of being at Shakri-La, on the sea couch with a cup of tea.

While snow floated down to the water's surface, I wrote:

> As snowflakes dissolve into the sea
> So, too, will this life.

The day slowly dimmed into twilight, and Woody had not come in. I expected he had gone off to Carolyn and Bob's. More and more lately, I wondered if I was good enough company for him. As Martini had said recently, "Dogs need friends, too. Sometimes we don't cut it."

Woody didn't seem to take to Shakri-La as he had to Hooverville and the Little Red Cabin. Part of it was the landscape—down a large hill that fronted a mostly rocky beach. Part of it was also my increased solitude. He was a pack animal, liked people and wanted more company. It seemed he had gotten a little bored with just me around. A few nights before, I had started to play *dog hockey* with him, but he had only tried haphazardly for the puck, looking at me with no fire in his eyes.

It was so cozy and beautiful and quiet, I decided to let him stay out overnight. Carolyn never seemed to mind, and Bob certainly didn't. The afternoon passed. Now and then, the ocean's surface rippled with a winter Chinook or the head of a seal looking up at Shakri-La. The White River wolf pack howled over the ridges above Woody Creek, their song cutting deep and lonely across the snowscape.

The next morning, I plugged in the phone and called Carolyn.

"How's the Wood dog?" I asked.

"I haven't seen him," Carolyn said.

A small, sharp, electric spasm jolted my midsection.

"You mean today? Have you seen him at all? I mean yesterday?"

"No, not since last week," she said matter-of-factly.

"Oh, shit. Oh, shit," I said. "Listen, I gotta go. Let me know if you see him, okay? He's been gone overnight. I just assumed he was with you."

My mind raced. I tried to think of people to call, but there was no one else. Carolyn's was the only place he ever strayed to. Otherwise, he had always come back on his own. I felt stupid and neglectful.

Up the snowy hill, I went looking for him. There, meeting me at the top, was the single set of dog prints leading away. Where to go? The most obvious was to drive along the highway and look for his inert frozen body off to the side. I was spared that horrible vision, however. The highway and ditches were deserted.

Down side roads and up dozens of driveways, I searched for dog tracks. Maybe someone had tied him up? He'd bark if he knew I was around. Many of these roads were new to me. I stopped often, walked around, and whistled. The notes sounded thin and desperate in the cold air, stretching to the edge of the trees absorbed by branch and snow. Some of the side roads went for a mile down to the ocean; some forked to other roads that led where? He could be anywhere. A desperate emptiness grew inside me.

As the day faded, the hope that he'd rush down to me from one of the nameless driveways dwindled as well. The only thing that had ever worked was to go home and to wait for him to come back. He always did. But at the top of the driveway, the only thing meeting me was the single set of tracks leading away. I called Martini and a half dozen other friends, who all promised to go out looking for him.

That night, it snowed again. Early the following morning, I kept looking at the phone, hoping it would ring. Up the hill again. New snow had obliterated the paw prints. I drove into town and placed an ad in the local paper, the *Ketchikan Daily News*. I used a picture that fine art photographer Hall Anderson had taken of Woody from Dr. Woody's Pet and Owner Look-Alike Contest that we did at the Blueberry Arts Festival. Woody, all triangle-eared and earnest, was looking down at us with a question in his eyes. Below it ran the text:

WANTED.
Woody the Dog.
For running away from home.
Reward. (907) 247-WOOF.

247-WOOF was my actual number. When the newspaper ad came out the next day, the telephone rang right off. A woman said she had seen a Labrador about six miles out of town as she drove by. I ran up the hill, heart almost busting from the deep snow, and drove to the address and knocked at the door. But they hadn't seen him, nor had any of the neighbors. Wandering around for a half hour more brought no luck.

Back home, a friend in Seattle told me of a dog psychic who helped people find lost pets by tuning in to the dog's whereabouts. Nothing felt too crazy right then. After describing him to her and telling her his name, the psychic was silent. "He is in a place that starts with an *S*," she said slowly.

The local vet had told me that dogs, especially purebreds like Woody, were sometimes stolen and taken out of state to be sold. So, I asked the psychic if he was still in Alaska. She paused again.

"Yes, I am getting that he is still in Alaska in a town that begins with *S*."

There was Sitka, Sterling, Soldotna, Seward, and Skagway. And then it hit me. *Oh my God. Saxman. He's in Saxman.* So once more, I huffed up to the road and drove the sixteen miles to Ketchikan and out the two and a half to Saxman. This made sense to me. Not sure how he would have gotten there, but Saxman was a place he could end up, a place with a few dogs who might have been his friends, plus some white and yellow mutts that could be his offspring.

I scoured the streets of Saxman, expecting to see him tied up in someone's yard, or maybe he was locked inside. I kept listening for his bark. Some of the Saxman kids followed along, calling out for Woody. Eventually, there were about ten of us. But after an hour, we gave up. Another dead end—and after each one, hope died a little more.

Wracked by guilt—had it been wrong to let him roam free in his life? One time, I had tied him up, to keep him around

Shakri-La, to see if it would cure him of his walkabouts. Maybe it would be better for him to have a more contained life, no longer allow him to be such a free dog, I thought. I rigged up a long wire that ran from the back porch to a hemlock tree sixty feet away. He could still wander from the beach over to the woods that fringed the waterfall, within reason.

I hooked on a swivel and a line with a clip for his collar, and the next time he wanted outside, I walked him over to the line and clipped him in. I showed him that he could walk around and that he had a range of fifty to sixty feet. He stood there looking at me like I was trying to sell him a Veg-O-Matic. Satisfied with my work, I turned to go inside, but felt his eyes dig into my back. I shut the door and went about my morning, working on a video project for the local schools.

An hour later, in the kitchen, partway through eating, I put the plate down. It was no use. The entire time inside, I had felt his eyes on me. I walked to the door—there he was, like a statue, not having moved a muscle, his eyes staring directly into mine.

I sighed, walked out, and bent down, unhooked the line, and said, holding his face, *You're right, amigo. I don't believe in doing this . . . and you know it.*

He wasn't meant to be a cooped-up dog, like some of the pitiful mutts tied to weather-beaten doghouses we'd see on our drives into town. They had gone slowly insane and then lay around in the dirt, their spirits broken. Or like big, energetic dogs in cities never allowed off their leash, their wild joy starved away.

Woody was meant to be free. Maybe it was irresponsible of me, but I just couldn't cage up his spirit, and he knew it. *So listen, amigo,* I said, staring into his big carrot-colored eyes. *Listen. You go free. Okay, you go free. But take care of yourself. Come back, okay. Always come back.* I hugged him to my chest, and he wagged his tail. As he wandered down to the beach that day, I prayed. I prayed to the angels who looked over him. I prayed to God and the masters who could hear me. I prayed that he be kept safe from harm, that he always be led home. And I trusted; I trusted in the universe.

Day five of his disappearance arrived. Beneath my anxiousness, there was still a strong belief in the reality of our reuniting. I saw it clearly; it would happen, the magical world would come through for us. For ten or fifteen minutes, many times during the day, I would meditate and send messages out to the universe, for Woody to find his way home.

His disappearance just didn't make sense. I knew we would live out our days together, an old, satisfied dog on a porch somewhere in a cabin with a family around him. The phone rang. There it was! I ran over and snatched it up midring.

"Hello!"

"Hi, is this Ward Serrill?"

My heart was about to burst with joy.

"Yes!"

"Mr. Serrill, my name is Michael Magula, and I am wondering how you feel about your life insurance coverage?"

"What?"

"Well, let me talk to you about the three reasons you should—"

"No, no, thank you!" I said and slowly pressed the hang-up button. I stood there, phone to my ear, listening to the drone on the line, while the ocean in front of Shakri-La lay like a ghost town.

I felt haunted by a moment from the night before Woody had disappeared. It was pitch-dark, seven o'clock, and we were driving from town to Shakri-La. Near the LP mill, I glanced over at him on the seat of the pickup. Instead of sleeping or looking out the window as usual, he was staring directly at me in the dark. In that instant, in the quick flashes of roadside lights, there had been something in his eyes. What was it? Those eyes held a mystery, a seriousness, a sense of gravity, a profound awareness.

I went to bed unable to pierce the mystery of that stare in the truck from the week before. In the middle of the night, I woke and in a waking dream state recalled that look—how he had been staring at me. There had been a *sadness* in his eyes, as if he were sensing the time to part had come, as if he were asking . . . *Why?* Maybe, in those eyes, he had been saying goodbye to me. My heart ached so deeply, I had to sit up in bed and hold my chest.

The next day, my friend Elsie called from Seattle. Elsie was in her seventies, ethereal and mystical. She was a great friend of Woody's from our occasional trips to Seattle. Whenever we came to town, we stayed at her and Max's enchanted farm in Kirkland, outside Seattle. She told me she had seen Woody in a vision. She said to keep a lookout for a man in a black pickup, that this man had negative energy and he had something to do with Woody's disappearance. I wondered if he had wandered into someone's yard one too many times, if some idiot with a gun had taken my heart away.

Turned out Woody was not just my dog. Dozens of people were out looking for him. Dr. Woody had become the most famous dog in Ketchikan. A woman in town told me that a lot of people were traumatized by his disappearance. On his own, he had formed all sorts of independent relationships with loggers, artists, fishermen, cannery workers, kids, cooks, teachers, librarians, bartenders, mill workers, carpenters, and grocery store clerks.

I slept downstairs on the couch that night, uneasily. The *whoosh* from the waterfall brought no comfort. Late in the dim dawn, a sound woke me. I lay in bed wondering what it was and then realized it had been a single paw scratch! I leapt up, ran through the kitchen, and threw the door open. Cold air and a few dead leaves met me. The only prints in the snow were from my own coming and going. I stood for some time as the cold sank into me. I had heard it. I was sure . . . *The scratch.*

Fitfully sleep finally came. The next morning, I couldn't stand up straight. My lower back had gone out, causing a thirty-degree forward bend to my torso. It took me a half hour to walk up the hill to my truck. The drive to the hospital was excruciating, and I checked myself into the emergency ward.

There I learned about the psoas muscle that runs from the front of the femur bone through the middle of the body where it attaches to the lumbar spine. It is a muscle so deep that it is virtually impossible to reach or massage. It traverses through the most vulnerable parts of our body, the waist, hips, groin, and belly. In some yogic traditions, it is the muscle associated with our deepest fears.

My hidden fear of Woody's loss and its grief had become physical. My left psoas muscle had gone into intense spasm and had exerted so much pressure that it buckled me over. The doctor gave me some muscle relaxants and sent me home. I wasn't able to drive, however, and went instead to a friend's house close to the hospital, where I spent days on her living room floor in a makeshift bed.

After recovering from the worst of my back spasms, I drove out to Shakri-La. It had now been nine days since Woody had left. The snow had nearly melted over the past week, and a light rain was falling. A week ago, the single set of dog tracks had disappeared under new snow. Now here they were again, as if by a cruel joke. The snow had melted inside the frozen tracks and exposed their shapes one more time. Rain ran through them. *A water dog.* His last tracks.

For the next week, the snow around the tracks slowly melted until they disappeared.

I never saw Woody the Dog again.

Chapter 45

NOT RUNNING

One can go off into the wilderness to hide or to find.
For you it would be grand to find yourself there, eh?
—Dr. Woody

When Woody left, so, too, did my faith—an abiding lifelong trust that everything would work out, that somehow a rabbit would always appear out of the hat. His departure dropped me onto the hard reality stones of Shakri-La. I lost faith in spirit, in God, in life, and in myself. There was no part of my reality that could even fathom our separation; it never entered my mind. When Woody was present, so, too, was a sublime confidence in my life and its direction. His disappearance made me realize I had no idea what was coming around the corner. That shook me to the core. What could I depend on? I had no tools to deal with the raw vulnerability of this question or of his loss.

There are those who hold that the most profound relationships in life are with other humans. We don't comprehend grief very well, especially when it comes to the loss of a dog. For many of us, an intimacy develops with an animal that is deeper than with humankind. In the private abiding innocence of the time with them and the unconditionally of their love, we often share with a dog what we can't as humans. We're more transparent about our feelings and vulnerabilities and more apt to show affection and even touch.

I've seen grown men who never cry bawl like babies when they lose a dog.

Even when we are alone, they are with us. Even when we forget them, there remains a silent, abiding bond. *A deeper intimacy.* A dog looks directly into your eyes; you see it when you enter a room, their eyes lock on yours. Eyes that look into you, consummating a secret, nonverbal communion. They communicate in a pure body language, without artifice. We may not realize how unfathomable the intimacy really was until they are gone, how deep the roots really went, how commonplace and necessary the connection.

We weren't ever alone.

Woody was the presence that encouraged me to risk and step away from a boxed-in existence, to go live in an abandoned cabin, to begin to explore the tapestry of nature, and pass through the doorway of solitude. With him gone, I was forced to face a stark aloneness. His departure inclined me to a place none of us go willingly, down the hill into the dominion of grief, where I could not run away.

Grief became the force that cracked me wide open, that broke through the armor around my heart. All the pain I had tried to hold in abeyance throughout my life now poured through relentlessly. My previous foray into solitude felt important yet flawed. Had I been hiding behind the mask of the dog, substituting him for deeper issues I was not facing? Had I used him to presume I didn't need human connection?

A new chapter in solitude had begun, one more challenging: a long walk back from the path of isolation. The grief at losing Woody initiated me into a more primitive healing cycle, one in which I had to face the accumulated losses of a lifetime. Woody's departure made me feel the tender, inevitable reality of aloneness and vulnerability, the true pain and fragility of life.

His leaving drove me to ask the most basic existential question: *Why am I here?* The answer took years to retrieve, but eventually this came: I am not here to get what I want or to lead a happy life or have my dreams realized. The most resonant truth that Woody's departure brought to me was this: *I am here to heal. And to express that into wholeness.*

That is enough.

EPILOGUE

Spring 2015

Dolly, our one-year-old yellow Lab, peered at me through the branches of the small cedar tree. In her mouth was her favorite toy, a multicolored stuffed parrot. Her eyes blazed with starlight. She was playing one of her best games, *tree hide*. It goes like this. She runs out and hides behind the limbs of a small tree. I am supposed to creep up close on the other side of it and be still until . . . suddenly racing around the tree to catch her! I am never close. She gallops away to another tree across the park and hides behind it to continue the game, which she can do all day.

Tree hide is one of the games she has invented, along with *queen of the hill*, where she runs to the top of a sawdust pile at a county park and battles me when I try to come up. Also, there is *soccer net*, where she waits behind a goal until I'm directly across from her and then she races around to jump on me with a growl. I can usually make it around the net once before getting tackled.

I didn't pick Dolly; she came through the Dog Star, Sirius. My wife, Sophie, and I had just come back from seeing the movie *Tracks*, the story of a lone woman's trek across Australia with her dog. Growing up, Sophie had never had a pet and saw for the first time via the film what having a relationship with a dog might look like. When we got home, she immediately went onto the internet to search for adoptions. Ten minutes later, she showed me a yellow Lab on her phone and said, "Here's our dog."

We picked her up that night from the shelter, a traumatized, seriously abused six-month-old puppy. On the ride home, Sophie sat in the dark in the back seat with her, and exclaimed in a hushed tone full of wonder, "Wardy, her head is on my lap!" It was her first direct contact with Dog.

Sophie started riffing on names. All our other animals were named after lady singers. Our cat, Mavis Staples, and our four chickens, Aretha Franklin, Bonnie Raitt, Emmylou Harris, and the skinny white one, Patti Smith. When Sophie suggested Dolly Parton, we both knew.

Just as it took years for Dolly to emerge from the extended trauma of her beginnings and rise into her own unique, autonomous, creative being, so, too, it has taken long years for me. Everyone I have ever known is wounded, and the journey of an authentic and true life involves turning to face that wound, with all its disappointments and struggle. But beneath that primal fracture lives the source of our greatest gift. Many years after losing Woody along with my faith in God and life, I began to develop a faith of a different kind. A trust that life would lead me to my greatest opportunity to heal—through acceptance, through forgiveness of myself, through experience.

Healing is a very patient master. *It takes all the time it needs.* And through it all, Woody has been here. I can feel him now, coming in the door with his free-roam, lithe, powerful body and joy shining eyes. When we love deeply, an energetic alliance is formed, lasting in its quality. It outlives the grave. Woody appears in dreams from time to time. Dolly has even become a sort of conduit to him. Mysteriously, when she hears the name Woody, her triangle ears pop up smartly; she listens keenly, intently, as if she is hearing a call of kinship.

It took a while for me to see Woody's greatest lesson. Looking back, in the gentlest, clearest way, Woody had been telling me all along that he was leaving. Even as a puppy, he would take off, many times for a few hours. Later, his absences grew to an afternoon, then longer until overnight, days, and eventually forever.

As my faultless mirror, my guide dog was showing me that all my life *I had been the one running away*. There is a fine line between leaving in pursuit of freedom and solitude, and running away from the pain and the truth in the depths of one's heart. I crossed that line and separated myself further and further into isolation. Woody's disappearance was a call to come home.

I believe that the greatest fear we have as humans is the fear of intimacy. True intimacy involves allowing others to see our naked pain. I feared the intimacy of anyone seeing my true aloneness and feelings of not belonging—the fear of a deep-down belief that I wasn't good enough to be loved. But I learned that you can't fully heal alone. While living in the Little Red Cabin, I received a letter from an Idaho farmer named George Crookham, grandpa of a friend of mine. George had listened patiently to my Icarus-driven young man dreams of freedom and wrote: *Someday, you might find a deeper freedom from* interdependency. I hadn't understood at the time. But we need others. Yes, time alone and excursions into solitude and flights toward freedom are helpful and, in my case, essential. Many are the manifold gifts to be found there. But true intimacy begins by reaching out, by a willingness to show our messy, vulnerable, afraid self. Therein lies a deeper freedom. The freedom to stand raw and held by self, others, and the world. To know our inherent belonging.

A more mature freedom is discovered through the interdependence of solitude and togetherness.

Woody the Dog was a retriever. He retrieved my heart, because it was inside and buried and, only through a great breaking, like a seed, could it truly emerge into life. Healing takes all the time it needs. *Sea time. Lighthouse time. Waterfall time. Dog-eyed time.*

I am home now.

I'd say more, but Dolly has just come up, the parrot toy in her mouth, carrot-colored eyes aimed directly at mine, a slow wag to her tail.

Go Outside! she tells me.

Addendum

CHEW THE BONE
WITH DR. WOODY

Dog was lonely; so he made Himself.
And he gave it four legs.
He gave it a long nose.
He gave it a tail
And sayeth unto him:

"Take thy stout, loyal heart—
Go Fetch Thyself."
—Lobo 1: 1–13

Dear Dr. Woody,

For ten years, I never stopped looking for you. I kept expecting you to come around the next corner all carrot joy-eyed and spring-limbed, or you'd be riding in the back of a pickup truck going by. Even visiting Seattle, I imagined seeing you walking with a new human around Green Lake. Hundreds of times, our reunion played out in my imagination. I memorized your little scars and injuries in case ever needing to prove in court that you were mine.

But you never came back. You never came back . . . Why did you leave?

—Wassy

Dear Wassy,
Dogs are angels in disguise and mirrors to two-leggeds. Why did I leave?
    —Dr. Woody

Dear Dr. Woody,
Maybe my heart had always been broken, but I armored it. And by leaving, always leaving, I wouldn't have to feel what was underneath.
    —Wassy

Dear Wassy,
Rebirth is a continuous process.
    —Dr. Woody

Dear Dr. Woody,
When you left, my heart broke open wide. It was like stone broken by the force of water. You were a water dog. You took me to a waterfall until my heart became it.
    —Wassy

Dear Wassy,
I always come back from where I left.
    —Dr. Woody

Dear Dr. Woody,
Is that where you are now?
    —Wassy

Dear Wassy,
Is that where you are now?
    —Dr. Woody

Dear Dr. Woody,
I am here. But where are you? James Taylor wrote a song called "Fire and Rain," and he sang about a friend he'd lost unexpectedly who he always thought he'd see again. What happened to you? My favorite story was that you went up in the woods and fell in love with a wolf bitch.
    —Wassy

Dear Wassy,
I left because I had other work to do. My next assignment was to be a guide dog for a blind woman. It's what I do. Help people see.
    —Dr. Woody,

Dear Dr. Woody,
But you said you always come back from where you left.
    —Wassy

Dear Wassy,
When you love, you are home.
    —Dr. Woody

Dear Dr. Woody,
When you would sleep, on your side sacked out on the floor, or hanging your jowls upside down from the mustard-colored armchair, you would often sob in your sleep. I always

wondered, were you crying for your mother, because I took you away from her?

—Wassy

Dear Wassy,
I cried because I miss you.
   —Dr. Woody

GRATITUDE

Where to begin? With my best pal, "Wag," Michael McMann, who understood Woody's Tao and, along with Les Killian, humored me with long musings about the Nature of Dog and Woody's watercourse way. To "Dog Lady," Patty Jones, who traveled with Woody and me on our inaugural Alaska voyage and shared intermittent, gentle lovings over the years. To "Arroz," Steven Rice, benefactor and armadillo wrangler, who deserves a credit as a co-producer on this *book-film*, by providing me endless support and critical financing along the way.

To "Coyote," Evan Albright, who gave me consistent, sage advice to help untie the most difficult knots in the story and encouraged me to look more deeply into the mirror. I hope he forgives me for cutting him out of the book. To developmental editor Marlene Blessing, who gave such astonishing insight and asked the hardest questions, all the while imbuing me with encouragement.

To Joseph Bednarik, co-publisher of Copper Canyon Press, who had the courage to tell me of an earlier draft that he thought it sucked; and while I didn't fully concur, his assessment inspired me to revise the next half dozen drafts.

To Brenda Peterson and her writing class, where some of the earliest chapters of this book emerged. Rikki Ducornet, who graciously read the first fifty pages and said nothing about the story but talked to me about style and eliminating as many *I*'s as possible, which is the best writing advice I've ever received. She also told me to "get to the heat sooner," which inspired me to cut out a lot of fluff.

To KRBD FM in Ketchikan, Alaska, and my cohort, Martini, who let me do crazy stuff and make wild and beautiful art over the airwaves and gave rise to *Chew the Bone with Dr. Woody*. And, of course, to VARC.

To June and Doug, who did their best and always wished for my happiness. They wounded me in profound and unique ways that stirred my deepest healings and becomings. Their raising of me also included countless sweetnesses and playings ("runny, runny weeeee") and duties of responsibility that this book, alas, could not contain.

To my siblings, Doug, Jim, and Merilee—each with their own uniquely different upbringing and experiences. To Grizzly, Coho, and Rat Ma—may you all grow up weirdly. To Jeanne "Quarter Stepmom" Serrill, for her support over many moons. To Stef and Alex, Ryan and Amy, Debbie, Cher, and Steven. To my spiritual grandparents, Max and Elsie Canterbury, who *saw* me when others couldn't. Who encouraged me to write and to believe in myself.

To David Goodenough, who guided me through a half dozen career and life changes. To my first mentor, Don Bunger, of Room 261 at Highline High School, who opened the magic door of creativity to me. I dedicate the chapter *"Freewoodsin'"* to him. To Michael Meade, for his life's work and help in finding my own true "gold" next to the wound.

To Dave Hunsaker, "Dancing Bear," and spiritual brother, who has encouraged me in countless ways as a most generous friend and artist. To my greatest (along with Buell) pen pal, Carolyn Stallings. For Lillian Ferrence, who fixed me with a serious gaze the last time I saw her and said, "You *must* write."

To Perry and Steve Reeve, for allowing me to live seven miraculous years at Shakri-La and to Bruce and Sher Schwartz who took over its stewardship after I left. To the people of

Saxman, who supported my efforts. I truly hope the appreciation of you can be felt amid and between the lines. To Ed Edelstein, who guided me in the architecture of creating a viable business for Saxman Cultural Village. To Forrest DeWitt Jr., Steve Williams, W. K. Williams, Craig Burger, Richard Shields Jr., Nathan Jackson, Martha Shields, Jeff Wold, Claudia Boyd, Jim Swink, and Ronni Sinnott for her work with the Saxman kids; Tom McGuire for his thankless efforts in developing the tribal house; and Joan Leighton for making the Village Store a success.

To Debrae Firehawk and Cara Faith and Eli Moch for essential wisdom council over the years. To Rocky Friedman, who besides creating the best little cinema in the country, The Rose Theatre, has served as a deep ally in more ways than he knows.

To *soul friends*, Jake "the Baptist" Farmer, Steven "Wek-Wek" Hay, Ken "Seawolf" Foster, Katherine "Josephine" Bragdon, David "Blind Lemon" Yeaworth, Cecile "Katgutz" Thomas, Lesley "Amoura" McClurg, Tim "Harrison" Harrington, Mary "Bird Lady" McAfferty, Mia Kelley, Eva "Bluegrass" Liljikvist, Pete Droge, Claytie Mason, Annalisa Barelli, Sara Rose, Eric Frith, Heather Carrie, Jackie Corning, and Deeji Killian.

To Dave Kifer, Ray Troll, Carolyn "Grandma" Minor, Bill Porter (Red Pine), Carolyn "Goof Mom" Michael, Janet Yoder, Vi Hilbert, Tricia LaRochelle, Elizabeth Kracht, Christine Hemp, Anna Quinn, Donna Kelleher, Lisa Pacot, Victoria Lord, Dr. Catherin Maxwell, Maureen Hoffman, Patricia Angel, Christine Burgoyne, Cim Edelstein, Shelley Goldstein, John Hoyt, Anne Tillery, Kristi Crookham, and George Crookham. To D.D. Wigley and Maria Mackey for their profound patronage of my work.

To Ted Kerasote for *Merle's Door*, Rick Bass for *Colter*, and Paul Auster for *Timbuktu*, and to Bob Dylan for blowing the top off my head with quicksilver language.

To all the folks at Girl Friday Books, The Little Engine That Could. Ingrid Emerick, publisher; Karen Upson, director, indie sales; Sara Spees Addicott, senior editor, book development; Dave Valencia, director, editorial production; Paul Barrett, art director; and Vanessa Campos, marketing strategist. To copyeditor Michelle Hope, proofreader Jenn Kepler, to Adrienne Robineau for the website, and to James Island, who was of essential help with images.

And last to Sophie Jane Hardy, who is most responsible for this book finally coming to manifestation. At the top of Mount Si in the Cascades, she abruptly stormed off down the trail as I moaned to her for the umpteenth time, "Yeah, if I had done that book about Woody . . ." I followed and looked for her around every bend and curve, even asking hikers on the way up if they had seen a tall brunette woman.

Hustling myself around a switchback, there she was barring my way. She scratched a line across the trail, and assuming Gandalf's imperial majesty, she drove her walking stick onto the path and proclaimed, "You, Regretful Writer, *shall not pass!*"

It was her refusal to let me pass that day that finally kicked me in the butt (sixty-one drafts ago).

And last—I hope this is not too corny—but thank you, oh Reader, for taking this journey with Woody and me. May it resonate and bring you closer to your heart and the four-legged friends around you.

ABOUT THE AUTHOR

Ward Serrill has written, directed, or produced over ninety short films and writing projects for progressive causes. His feature-length film, *The Heart of the Game*, shot over seven years, debuted at the Toronto International Film Festival in 2005 and was released nationally by Miramax Films in 2006. The film won high praise across the country from the likes of Jay Leno, Ebert and Roeper ("an Oscar level piece of work"), *People Magazine, USA Today, O Magazine, Rolling Stone*, and others. He was executive producer for *Wild America*, narrated by Sissy Spacek, and he codirected and produced *Building One House*, narrated by Robert Redford. Ward's other documentaries include *The Bowmakers*, the story of the most important instrument you've never heard of; *Song of the New Earth*, about the power of sound; *Catching Fire*, on Peter Scott, developer of a cook stove to save lives and forests in the developing world; *Babies Behind Bars*, for Soledad O'Brien; and *TreeStory*, about humanity's relationship to trees. He is currently working on his fourth feature film, *Dancing with the Dead: The Life and Times of Red Pine*. Ward taught advanced nonfiction film at Cornish College of the Arts in Seattle. He lives in Port Townsend, Washington, dances tango, and plays harmonica. To contact him or listen to his podcast, *Chew the Bone with Dr. Woody*, go to wardserrill.com.

CPSIA information can be obtained
at www.ICGtesting.com
Printed in the USA
JSHW021020120921
18621JS00008B/8